ROSS PEROT

What does he stand for?

Contributing Writers

Jacob Drake
Carri Karuhn
Joyce Werges

"Perot's Vision of America"
Story and interview by Chris Tucker

PUBLICATIONS INTERNATIONAL, LTD.

Contributing writers

Jacob Drake is a freelance writer and a news editor in the Chicago metropolitan area.

Carri Karuhn is business editor for a suburban Chicago newspaper chain.

Joyce Werges is a freelance writer and assistant managing editor for a Chicago-area newspaper chain.

Chris Tucker has covered Ross Perot frequently through features and recent interviews in his capacity as executive editor and columnist for *D Magazine*, the city magazine of Dallas and Fort Worth. Tucker's monthly column, "Sense of the City," is about social and political issues, and he is a regular commentator for National Public Radio.

Special acknowledgment to Joan Dobson, Mike Smith, Marcia Dellenbach, Mary Wahlgren, Carol Keeley, and William Marsh for their research assistance.

Photo Credits

AP/Wide World Photos: 18, 40, 45, 58, 68, 76, 81, 85, 86, 89, 93 (bottom), 137, 147; **Bettmann Archives:** Reuters: 176; UPI: 27, 72, 83, 91, 93 (top), 95, 143; **Black Star:** Dennis Brack: 152; Phil Huber: 32, 52; Shelly Katz: 21, 36, 60, 156; Barbara Laing: 64, 56, 178; Rob Nelson: 111, 149; John Chaisson: 48, 62; Ed Culwell: 144; **Index Stock Photography, Inc.:** front cover (background); **Picture Group:** Bob East III: 103; Jim Knowles: 132; Roger Sandler: 175, 188; Gerald Schumann: back cover, 106; Pete A. Silva: 98, 101, 172, 180, 182, 183, 184, 185, 186, 187, 189, 190, 191, 192; **Sipa-Press:** Hussein Akhtar: 59, 66, 70; David Sams: 6, 9, 12, 14, 15; **Sygma:** Eddie Adams: front cover, 114, 125; F. Lee Corkran: 129; Bob Daemmrich: 119.

CONTENTS

DISCOVERING ROSS PEROT

"I don't feel I'm any different from most Americans, except that I have a great deal of independence. I have the time and the funds to do what I do."—Ross Perot
Newsweek; December 1, 1980

There is something peculiarly American about the myth of the noble outsider—the high-minded stranger who arrives, seemingly from nowhere, to clean up the town and make things right.

Maybe that's part of the appeal of Ross Perot, the Texas billionaire who wants to be President of the United States. To be sure, Perot's own life story is the very stuff of American myth: humble beginnings; military service; crackerjack sales career with IBM; a business of his own; eventual billionaire status. Ross Perot is the American Dream personified.

He's also a philanthropist who supports the arts and sciences; a zealous reformer of public education; and a hard-nosed commander in the war against drugs. He's a self-styled "doer," not a "sayer."

Now, riding the groundswell of enthusiastic grass-roots support and with enough money to mount an effective campaign, Perot is making a bid for the highest office in the land.

He claims to disdain what he calls the "stunts, sound bites," and "dirty tricks" of modern presidential campaigning. He has a point, but his wealth will not protect him from the need to play the political game, nor will it shield him from the scrutiny that must be endured by any campaigner. Indeed, by mid-May 1992, the media had begun to get tough with Perot, and to take a hard look at his personal and business lives. The coverage will not become more merciful as the campaign progresses. The manner in which Perot—and the American public—react to that coverage will play a major part in the outcome of the billionaire's quest for the presidency.

In the meantime, *Ross Perot: What does he stand for?* will help introduce this plain-talking, monumentally ambitious man to the public he is so eager to serve.

CHAPTER 1

THE EARLY YEARS

"I love the ordinary people. I was one of them. Still am. I just got lucky."—Ross Perot
Dallas Morning News; May 3, 1992

Opposite: Flanked by his mother, Lulu (left), and his wife, Margot, Ross Perot graduates from Annapolis in 1953.

His beginnings were what some might call humble.

Henry Ross Perot was born June 27, 1930 in Texarkana, Texas, the youngest of two children. His father, Ross, was a rough-hewn cotton broker, as had been his father before him. Perot's mother, Lulu Ray, was a lumber company secretary turned homemaker.

Although far from wealthy, the Perots weren't as poor as many in Depression-era east Texas. The children had access to private educations at the Patty Hill School, where academic study was spiced with the reading of Bible verses. Although the school enforced a strict code of discipline, it also encouraged each student's creative expression. So it was that young Ross Perot learned how to think and how to behave.

Perot credits his parents, and simple luck, for many of the successes he has had in his life. He remarked in a March 18, 1992, C-SPAN interview, "People have asked me over the years, 'How did it suddenly feel after years and years and years of having a modest life to realize you were rich?' My reply is, 'I was born rich because of the two parents I had.' No child could have had two better parents than my sister and I had. That's so much more important than any financial wealth."

Perot recognized that each parent had qualities he could learn from and emulate. While discussing his father during the C-SPAN

Perot was born into modest surroundings. From the start, he was an ambitious boy with a strong sense of fair play.

interview, Perot remembered, "I got to sit in his office and watch him do business with the farmers. He was a wonderful man. He was a very kind and decent man. His philosophy was never take advantage of the farmer because he works hard all year to produce a bale of cotton. The broker buys it and sells it to the mills. Treat the farmer fairly and he will come back to you year after year. A pretty good thing to teach a little boy."

Perot's mother, too, made a deep impression on him. "She was a tiny little lady," he told C-SPAN. "We lived five blocks from the railroad tracks. The hobos would come off the train during the Depression, up the little dirt road past our house, and again and again and again, they would come to our back door and ask for food. While we didn't have a whole lot, she always gave them food. I'll never forget one day a hobo came up and took the food and said, 'Lady, do you have a lot of people come here?' She said, 'Yes.' He said, 'Come out here and I'll show you why.' Right at the edge of the road was a mark. He said, 'You see that? You're a mark.' After he left, I said, 'Mother, do you want me to get rid of that?' She said, 'No. These are good people. They're just like us, but they're down on their luck. We should help them.' Now in a thousand ways she taught me that by example—not by lecture, by example."

Besides his activities as a cotton broker, Perot's father bought and sold horses, keeping them in a vacant lot across the street from the family home. Those horses provided young Ross with his first paying job: When the boy was seven, his father paid him a dollar for each horse he broke.

Before long Perot began his entrepreneurial career. Like many other kids across America, he sold garden seeds and he sold Christmas cards. Early on, though, his energy and sense of fair play set him apart from other boys. The earliest of the many legendary stories about Perot involves the newspaper route he maintained for the Texarkana *Gazette.* As the story goes, Perot approached the *Gazette* circulation department with an offer to establish a route in the city's black ghetto. Perot told the paper that a route in this untapped territory should be worth a higher rate than that made by other carriers. The paper supposedly agreed, assuming that the youngster's efforts wouldn't amount to much. But soon the aggressive young salesman was making upwards of $25 every week. This was a considerable sum at the time, so the *Gazette* cut Perot's pay rate to what the other carriers were making.

But Perot would have none of that. As legend has it, the boy went to the publisher of the newspaper, described to him the deal he had struck with the circulation department, and insisted that the *Gazette* was unethically trying to renege. The publisher, charmed (or perhaps just startled) by the boy's nerve, agreed to maintain Perot at the higher pay rate.

At age 12, Perot decided to join the Boy Scouts. A member of Texarkana's Troop 18, he applied the same determination and spirit he used when breaking horses and selling papers. Within 16 months, he made Eagle Scout. Perot's scouting experience is a seminal one in his life, and instilled in him many of his ideas about service to one's country.

Paradoxically, perhaps, Perot was never a high-visibility student. In the 1992 C-SPAN

Never an outstanding student, Perot spent much of his youth absorbed in the care and training of horses.

interview he recalled a high school English teacher, Mrs. Grady Duck: "She said, 'Ross, it's a shame you're not as smart as your friends.' I said, 'Mrs. Duck, I am as smart as they are, but they just study all the time.' Mrs Duck said, 'Ross, talk is cheap.' That really got to me."

Henceforth, Perot applied himself to his studies and eventually achieved an academic standard that made him eligible for admission to the U.S. Naval Academy at Annapolis. But Perot remained in Texarkana for two years after high school before he finally found a member of Congress who would sponsor his appointment.

In the interim, Perot attended Texarkana Junior College, where he got his first taste of leadership after being elected President of the Student Council in his second year. He took his duties seriously and was soon lobbying the city's Chamber of Commerce and school officials, urging them to build a larger campus.

Perot explained to C-SPAN, "They had decided to build a new junior college right across the street from the present junior college on a square block of land. I and the other students felt that was a great mistake and they should build a bigger campus so the college could grow. I took a pretty good level of heat for even saying anything. But we were able to build a consensus . . . that the college should be moved, and it was moved to a 90-acre campus.

"I learned several things here—that you should stand up for what you believe in. Number two, if you do, expect to get cut up." Perot added that the experience taught him not to fret about his image.

Perot was granted his appointment to Annapolis in 1949; his Congressional sponsor was Senator W. Lee O'Daniel.

Annapolis brought out Perot's latent qualities of leadership. The disciplined young man flourished under the regimentation of the academy and after the end of his first year was ranked by his classmates, upperclassmen, military officers, and academic officers as first in his class in leadership.

While an upperclassman, he was elected president of his class. In that office, he was instrumental in the creation of a student court that heard charges of misconduct by students.

Perot's class numbered about 1,000, and by graduation he ranked at about the midpoint of the group. He spent the first two years of his active Navy service aboard the destroyer USS *Sigourney*, where he rose to the post of chief engineer.

The Navy gave Perot the opportunity to see and experience many of the places that he, like most other schoolchildren in east Texas, had only read and dreamed about. In his first nine months of duty, he saw the world.

Newly commissioned in the U.S. Navy and flanked by his loved ones, Perot beams for the camera.

The optimistic Perot clashed with an allegedly unethical superior while in the Navy, and became disillusioned.

But Perot's naval career was not all smooth sailing. When the commander of the *Sigourney* was transferred, Perot suddenly found himself with a new commander, a man with whom he clashed over matters of ethics. Perot abruptly found himself transferred to an aircraft carrier, the USS *Leyte,* and reduced to gunnery control. Later, he apparently put his career disappointment aside and became an assistant navigator.

Perhaps happiness in his personal life helped him overcome what some observers might call a military-career failure. In 1956 Perot married Margot Birmingham, a college student he met on a blind date while at Annapolis. The ceremony took place in Margot's western Pennsylvania hometown of Greensburg, following her graduation from Goucher College, near Baltimore.

The couple eventually had five children— Ross, Jr., Nancy, Suzanne, Carolyn, and Catherine, who now range in age from 21 to 34.

Today, Perot looks to his children as a measure of his success. If they've turned out well, it has been partly due to his insistence that they never let their wealth go to their heads. In an interview published in the October 27, 1987, issue of *Forbes,* Perot recounted a lesson he taught Ross., Jr., at the age of 12. He had hired the boy to plant bushes around the fence at the edge of his company's property. In return, Ross, Jr., would be paid 35 cents for each bush.

"That seemed like a pretty good price," Perot remembered, "—until [Ross, Jr.] hit rock. Now he's in real estate development and every time he has a project, the first thing he does is check for rock."

Perot felt it was important to teach his children not just the value of a dollar but a sense of moral responsibility. He feels he and his wife did a good job with their children. He told the C-SPAN interviewer about a time when Ross,

Jr., then a second lieutenant in the Air Force, had been recommended by a sergeant as one of America's ten outstanding young men. Perot said his son accepted the news of the selection graciously, telling his father, "'I want that sergeant sitting right next to you when I get it.'"

"Now there's a kid with his head straight," Perot said approvingly.

Perot obviously takes great pride in his son's accomplishments. Although his own naval career did not pan out as he had hoped, it did give him the opportunity to get into the business world and amass the fortune that today makes him one of the richest men in the United States.

While an assistant navigator, Perot met an IBM executive who was attached to the Naval Reserve. The executive liked Perot's style and suggested he contact the company about a position. Perot was intrigued. While still in the Navy, he took IBM's tests, passed, and was contacted by the corporation's Dallas office to come in for an interview. When his tour was up in 1957, Perot resigned his commission. He and his young wife packed all their worldly possessions in a 1952 Plymouth and hit the road for Texas. Perot was about to begin a period of remarkable personal and professional growth.

CHAPTER 2

HOME-GROWN BILLIONAIRE

"A businessman has a duty to his employees, his company, and his country. He must make that company successful, so it can add necessary jobs and broaden the nation's tax base. That's how private companies help the government cover its functions."
—Ross Perot
Saturday Evening Post; April 1983

Opposite: Ross Perot—showing off a new piece of technology in 1968—started EDS at age 32 after IBM turned down his idea.

When Ross Perot left the United States Navy for the world of business, he traded in his peacoat for a necktie and suit, but he never shed the militaristic approach to life he had learned while attending the Naval Academy at Annapolis.

Perot began his business career in 1957 at the age of 27 selling computers for IBM. From the beginning, he made a name for himself in the computer industry. All of his four years with IBM were marked with extraordinary success. The young salesman filled his annual sales quota earlier and earlier each year, until gradually he was accepting more and more contracts.

"I was very successful as an IBM salesman," Perot told *Newsweek*. (April 27, 1992.) In 1962, Perot filled his annual sales quota only 19 days into the year. But, he later told *Newsweek*, it had nothing to do with his selling abilities. "It had everything to do with selling umbrellas when it's raining. It was the beginning of the computer industry," Perot said. "Everybody was buying computers."

According to Perot, stories that circulated about his extraordinary salesmanship can be summed up in a few short words, "I worked all day." Because of the demand for computers at the time, it was possible to sell a quota in a half-day. If a salesman worked all day, Perot told *Newsweek* in the same article, "you could run up quite a record."

Ross Perot in his office in 1986; note the painting "Spirit of '76" on the wall behind him.

Then IBM made its first mistake as far as Perot was concerned. Because of his success selling computers, the company capped his commissions.

Perot had time on his hands and nothing to do. Realizing that the computer age was new and that many of his customers had little working knowledge of the setup or operation of these machines, Perot proposed establishing a division that would provide customized software for his clients. The division would even make technicians available to operate the computers.

And then IBM made its second mistake with Perot. When he presented the idea to IBM, the company turned him down, saying the plan would never be successful because the market was too small. Perot believed otherwise. He quit IBM and, on his 32nd birthday (June 27, 1962), founded Electronic Data Systems Leasing Company (EDS) with $1,000, which was the minimum required to incorporate under Texas state law.

According to *Newsweek* (April 27, 1992), Perot's wife, Margot, supplied him with the initial stake, which she had earned from her teacher's salary of $300 a month. "So, Margot's $1,000 started EDS," said Perot. "That's the only capital that went into EDS until it went public in 1968."

Many years later, Perot related a story to *Newsweek* about Margot's contribution to the company. "Margot has no interest in money, couldn't care less," he said. "Years go by, and one night she asked in a very sweet voice, 'Will you explain something to me? If I put all the money into EDS, why does half of it belong to you?'" Perot told *Newsweek* he was probably "the only man in Texas who ever enjoyed explaining community property to his wife."

When his son, Ross Perot, Jr., was born, Perot recalled, "I bought Margot a $1,000 string of pearls. That was all I had in the bank. If she could just keep one piece of jewelry, guess which one she'd keep."

The concept behind Perot's one-person business was similar to what he had presented to IBM. EDS would function as an on-site data-processing facility programming computers and designing software to meet the needs of individual clients. EDS also would maintain and operate the entire computer system.

Although Perot's brainstorm was innovative and seemingly practical for the industry, he had difficulty finding investors. "The story of my net worth is that everybody thought the idea was so bad, nobody wanted to invest in it," he told *Newsweek*. (April 27, 1992.) This situation proved profitable, since it avoided diluting his stock.

"When I was getting started, if anybody had offered me money for my EDS stock, he would have gotten it in a minute," Perot told *Newsweek*. (November 2, 1987.) "But everybody thought I had such a rotten idea I couldn't sell my stock."

Perot had few expenses his first years of business. Rent was $100 a month, and he only had one employee his first four months, secretary Betty Smith. In fact, the company's biggest outlay was its telephone bill. Perot made calls all over the country trying to interest potential clients in his service. But the entrepreneur was not without a cash flow. Income came from an annual salary from IBM, part-time work for Blue Cross, and his wife's teaching salary.

According to Todd Mason's book, *Perot, An Unauthorized Biography,* Perot landed his first account after 78 unsuccessful telephone calls.

His 79th was to Collins Radio Company in Cedar Rapids, Iowa. Collins needed to expand on its computer time for a major software development.

Then, as if wanting to teach IBM a lesson, Perot declared a competitive war on IBM. He not only persuaded an IBM client to cancel an order and contract with EDS, but he also recruited some of IBM's top employees.

The company Perot stole away from IBM was Frito-Lay. According to *Perot, An Unauthorized Biography,* Frito-Lay had been struggling for two years to develop a sales route for their accounting system. Perot, known for his results-oriented sales pitch learned from IBM, convinced the firm to contract with EDS. To handle the account, Perot recruited some of IBM's top employees, including Jim Cole, the senior technical man in the IBM Dallas branch; IBM engineers Thomas Downtain and Cecil L. Gunn; and others.

Perot refused to credit himself for anything beyond developing the deal. "My financial success rests squarely on the fact that we have an incredibly talented team of people [at EDS]," he told the February 16, 1986, Dallas *Morning News.*

Perot revels in the glory days of his small company's battles against IBM, said the Dallas *Morning News* in the same article. His employees would "scale the cliff" to beat IBM at every turn. Even the smallest details, including the personal appearance of salesmen, helped turn EDS into the largest computer services company in the country.

Making Perot's conquests even sweeter was his admiration for the way IBM conducted business. He told *U.S. News & World Report* (June 20, 1988) he credited his success to the principles of good business IBM taught him. "I saw IBM's emphasis on quality," he said. "Tom Watson was a master at motivating his people, at recognizing and rewarding excellence. If it hadn't been for his great company, no one would ever have heard of me." That is why, he told the Dallas *Morning News* (February 16, 1986), "nothing feels better than winning against a team like that."

Perot liked to hire only the best of the best for any of his endeavors, he told *Texas Monthly*. (December 1988.) "I want people who are smart, tough, self-reliant, have a history of success since childhood, a history of being the best at what they've done, people who love to win. . . . And if you run out of people who love to win, look for people who hate to lose." In other words, Perot was looking for people like himself.

His methods for hiring employees and running a business were far from standard. Perot demanded complete loyalty, and if an employee quit, he or she was often regarded as a traitor.

"He's supersmart, and he doesn't look for 'yes people,'" a former associate told *Newsweek*. (April 27, 1992.) "But don't try to argue with him twice on the same basis—he'll throw you out of his office. When he gets an idea fully formed, it's done."

Perot ran EDS in a paramilitary fashion, recalling his days in the Navy. He liked to hire war veterans. He implemented a strict dress code requiring men to wear dark suits, white shirts, and conservative ties. Neither facial hair nor tasseled shoes were permitted. Women wore skirts or dresses unless temperatures outside reached freezing.

Perot's standard of excellence extended beyond physical appearance. According to the October 31, 1983, issue of *Fortune* magazine, employees signed a code of ethics promising to conduct themselves "in the center of the field of ethical behavior, not along the sidelines."

Divorces were frowned upon, and extramarital affairs could be grounds for dismissal. If caught discussing one's salary with others, pilfering company goods, or using illegal drugs or alcohol at work, employees could consider themselves out of a job.

According to the December 1988 *Texas Monthly,* as part of his indoctrination of new employees into the corporate culture, Perot often sent them to intense training camps. "What is an EDSer?" Perot asked rhetorically. "An EDSer

Perot's success is partly due to his hard work. He expected the same from his employees: long hours with low pay.

is a person that goes anywhere, anytime, 24 hours a day, seven days a week, to make sure that EDS is the finest computer company in the world and that nobody beats us in competition."

This work environment may appear stuffy and uptight to some, but Perot never felt that way. The August 8–21, 1984, *Financial World* quoted a *Wall Street Journal* report that upset

Perot because it compared Perot's work force with "followers of the Reverend Sun Yung Moon because his employees seemed blindly devoted to their leader despite unusually rigid work loads and low salaries."

"That was the ultimate cheap shot," Perot told *Financial World.* "It had absolutely no relevance and is totally inaccurate." In fact, he said, "My family and friends get amused when they read that I'm severe because they think I have a great sense of humor and am rather informal."

EDS struggled through its first four years, and Perot continued to demand total commitment and loyalty from his employees. Hours were long and pay was low. And although Perot stressed the importance of the family, his employees rarely saw their families.

"'Whatever it takes' became shorthand for working 14-hour days and crawling back to a hotel room that had been home for five months," wrote Mason in *Perot, An Unauthorized Biography.* Perot's management style never would have worked if Perot had not hired dedicated employees who prided themselves in accomplishment, Mason said.

The dedication and loyalty of the employees did not go unnoticed or unappreciated. One evening, while all his employees were attending a black-tie affair held in their honor, Perot went to the home of every employee. "He had visited each of their wives to thank them for their patience and to present them with 100 shares of EDS stock, worth $400,000 25 years later," Mason wrote.

If an employee faced a crisis, Perot was there to do what he could. When an employee's baby was born with a congenital heart defect in a New York City hospital, wrote Mason, "Perot rounded up his neighbor, a heart surgeon, to take command of the emergency from Dallas." The infant underwent surgery and lived.

Mason recounts another instance. When the wife of future EDS president and loyal friend Mort Meyerson accidentally splashed drain cleaner in her eye, Perot found a "top ophthalmologist" to treat her.

Nothing, however, can compare with the daring rescue he organized when two EDS employees were taken hostage in Iran during the Khomeini revolution in 1978–79. EDS had been working on a $41 million contract with Iran to computerize that nation's social security and health care records. According to *Fortune* (October 31, 1983), Perot sent a team of EDS employees to free his two men when the two were jailed over a dispute concerning the contract; in the process, the prison was stormed by a mob, freeing some 13,000 captives (other sources say 11,000 captives), including Perot's two men.

EDS and its dedicated employees persevered through its first four years of business. Then came the big break.

Congress legislated two health insurance programs in 1965—Medicaid and Medicare—opening the door for Perot to lay a cornerstone for his future empire. The programs, mandated and partly paid for by the federal government, were operated by each of the 50 state governments through contracts with private insurance firms such as Blue Cross and Blue Shield.

Underestimating the health care demands of its pensioners, the Social Security Administration discovered the insurance industry was swamped with Medicare claims. "Half of Congress was up in arms because their elderly constituents were being hounded by bill collectors for claims Medicare had yet to pay," wrote Mason. "The other half was outraged about the cost of Medicare and the mounting evidence of fraud."

Into this quandary stepped Perot with an opportunity to use the technology rejected by IBM to sort the nation's health care records while at the same time making an immense profit for fledgling EDS. EDS took on the responsibility of computerizing the process of paying the large amount of incoming Medicaid and Medicare claims. The process proved so successful that by 1966 EDS's profits were eight times larger than the year before.

Perot took EDS public in September 1968, and the stock was an instant success. Almost overnight, Perot's 81 percent share of the company skyrocketed to $220 million. Within 18 months, that figure grew to $1.5 billion—all from government contracts and his computer software idea that IBM rejected.

Ramparts Magazine hailed Perot as the "Welfare Billionaire," a man who made his fortune off the medical bills of the needy via the U.S. government. And while the "welfare billionaire" tag stuck, Perot always owned up to the fact he owed a great debt to the United States for his success.

With his software programming now a demonstrated success, competition began to grow. IBM, finally realizing the potential, was moving into the market.

Although Perot would later attribute much of his success to IBM, he still maintained a personal goal of never letting IBM forget they had turned down the opportunity of a lifetime. He was intent on showing IBM leaders that they had made a grave error.

Perot stepped up his efforts to steal business from IBM. He started by recruiting many of IBM's top employees. Then he developed a merit pay system for the sales staff: cash and stock bonuses for any employee who successfully wrestled a contract away from IBM.

Suddenly finding himself a billionaire, Perot resisted any changes in personality. The hours were still long and his demands remained high. And of course, the codes of conduct remained in place. Perot also never lost his ability to

Despite his wealth, Perot ate lunch in the EDS cafeteria
with other employees, who called him "Ross."

"identify" with his employees. In the company
cafeteria, where Perot ate with the rest of the
workers, he was addressed by all as "Ross." To
keep personal incentives high, Perot maintained
an annual salary of $68,000 a year with no
bonuses. If Perot relied on EDS dividends for his
livelihood, he would maintain constant pressure
for growth and success.

EDS continued to prosper through the end of
the 1960s and into the 1970s. By 1971, Perot
had amassed quite a personal fortune, and a
reputation.

When the brokerage firm of du Pont, Glore
Forgan & Company took a nose dive and
threatened to take Wall Street down if the firm

went under, Perot was called for help. He was willing and capable of making such a large financial move, and he could use his demonstrated leadership abilities to save the company.

In the February 23, 1987, issue of *Barron's*, Perot stated, "I was encouraged by virtually everybody at a senior level in government in Washington, and certainly by everybody at a senior level in Wall Street, and certainly by everybody running a major New York bank, to step in to avoid what they perceived to be an impending disaster, because there was no specific legislation to bail out a failing firm."

Perot said he was told if he did not save du Pont, the stock market would collapse. Reluctantly, he agreed, but only after "Nixon aides 'got down on their hands and knees' and insisted that saving the firm was necessary to avoid a financial disaster on Wall Street," according to the May 8, 1992, edition of the Chicago *Tribune*.

Responding to a call for help from Nixon did not surprise many people. At the time, Perot and President Nixon had a close relationship. Nixon had used Perot in the past to assist in the fight for better treatment of American POWs in Vietnam. At Nixon's behest, Perot even spent $4 million of his own money in an attempt to embarrass the North Vietnamese government. According to the Chicago *Tribune* article, Perot was in regular contact with the White House (sometimes as often as once a week), attended White House social affairs, and had requested and received three private meetings with the President.

But Perot also had a personal stake in the success or failure of du Pont. EDS had been performing du Pont's data processing, and the account generated about 10 to 12 percent of EDS's revenues, according to *Barron's*. (February 27, 1987.)

What began as a $5 million investment, the maximum amount Perot was told it would take to save du Pont, continued to grow. By the time Perot gave in to defeat and admitted he would not be the Wall Street savior this time, du Pont was in Chapter 11 proceedings and Perot was out $60 million.

Perot was not known as a regular player in the stock market, preferring to invest in safer government bonds. When asked his impression of Wall Street after the du Pont failure, Perot told *Barron's*, "I don't have any problems with Wall Street. I was trying to farm when there wasn't any rain."

There are some who believe Perot could possibly have saved du Pont had he not tried to make it into another EDS. His attempt to remake the company into a paramilitary "mold" of EDS was another reason for the failure of du Pont, wrote Mason in *Perot, An Unauthorized Biography*.

"Perot lectured long and often on the Street's short-comings," stated Mason. "His ideas were good ones, but they didn't win converts or business."

Although Wall Street did not crash as some predicted when du Pont closed, Perot had other problems. EDS lost some major insurance-processing contracts. Earnings leveled off and EDS's stock price fell to $2.75 a share, according to *Fortune.* (October 31, 1983.)

Du Pont's failure may have been a defeat for Perot, but generally he was not the type of man to give up a fight.

In 1970, Perot wanted to move his corporate headquarters to a residential area in Dallas. But when the Dallas City Council rejected his request for office zoning, stated *Texas Monthly* (December 1988), Perot threatened the city by saying he would move the company entirely out of Dallas. The zoning was passed the following year, and Perot kept EDS in Texas.

EDS continued to grow and so did Perot's personal fortune. The 1970s were filled with business and personal adventures, and Perot was at the wheel steering all the way. By 1979, Perot decided it was time to concentrate on other activities. He named Mort H. Meyerson president and turned daily corporate operations over to him. Meyerson was a trusted and long-time employee who received much of the credit for EDS's growth and huge financial success.

His EDS office may look plush (note the Remington bronzes), but Perot does not live an extravagant lifestyle.

Perot remained active in the corporate jungle, especially when there was a fight to be won. He moved from one conquest to another, refusing to accept "no" for an answer and rising to meet any challenger head on.

One of those challengers attacked in 1980. Texas Medicaid voted unanimously to accept a bid from Bradford National of New York over EDS to handle the state's data processing needs. According to the state, Bradford offered a contract that would save Texas $20 million over four years.

Perot was incensed, more from the thought of losing the contract of his home state that he had held for so many years than from the sheer money. Upon hearing the news, Perot promptly flew home from a vacation in Europe to meet privately with three Texas welfare agency board members. Perot insisted the savings figures were incorrect.

Although his own advisers recommended cutting his losses, Perot continued his blitz on the board members. According to *Texas Monthly* (December 1988), the board of the Texas welfare agency revoked its unanimous decision after two weeks. Eventually, the health insurance firm rebid the contract and negotiated a one-year renewal with EDS. Bradford declined to rebid, instead accepting a $3.1 million settlement from the state.

After securing the Texas contract, one of his most prized accounts, Perot's next big corporate success came in the form of a government contract in 1981 called Project Viable.

Project Viable, according to *Fortune* (October 31, 1983), was an Army program designed to replace outdated "IBM mainframe computers doing administrative record-keeping chores" on 47 Army bases around the country.

Computer Sciences, Inc., one of EDS's top competitors, was the government's front-runner for the contract. Adding to the interest in the situation was Computer Sciences' subcontractor: IBM.

Perot wanted that contract. According to *Fortune*, IBM and Computer Sciences planned to replace the government's outmoded computers with smaller, more efficient, and more powerful machines. But Perot saw that his company's system was less expensive and that he could provide a backup for any data base that malfunctioned. Perot jumped at the chance, and in April 1982 the Army bestowed the ten-year, $656 million contract upon EDS.

Around the time Perot was securing the Army account, corporate giant General Motors was trying to pick up the pieces after one of its worst years, losing $763 million in 1981. General Motors was making some changes, and GM chairman Roger Smith was behind it all.

"I'm not a guy who likes change," Smith was quoted in the June 17, 1985, issue of *Newsweek*, "but we have to change."

One of Smith's attempts at streamlining his operation involved searching for a more efficient computer system. With more than 100 mainframe computers scattered throughout its plants, GM used more computers than any other conglomerate. But the computers were not operating efficiently, and Smith began shopping for a data-processing firm to take over that end of the business. According to *Newsweek*, "Many of them [the mainframes] duplicate functions of others and there are serious gaps; design computers, for example, cannot communicate directly with production."

Since EDS was the expert in reorganizing computer systems, Smith approached Perot with an idea. Smith wanted to purchase EDS and merge the two companies into one corporate conglomerate.

EDS would revamp GM's computer system, consolidating its data-processing and becoming "the central nervous system of GM, linking engineers with designers, salesmen with executives, robots with computers" stated the June 17, 1985, *Newsweek.*

But Perot was skeptical about the deal, and EDS president Mort Meyerson was uncertain. "I laughed," Meyerson told *Newsweek* when Perot told him about GM's offer. "I said, 'You mean GE, don't you?'"

Despite these doubts, the two companies announced the purchase of EDS by GM for $2.55 billion in August 1984. Through the deal, Perot, who owned 46 percent of EDS's 58 million outstanding shares, pocketed $1.2 billion for himself.

The merger would begin "a new era of opportunity for EDS," Perot told the Dallas *Morning News.* (October 19, 1984.) "EDS has always been a company that has looked forward," Perot said. "From our view, we just signed the world's biggest customer."

Under the acquisition agreement, Perot stayed on at EDS's Dallas headquarters, but reported directly to Smith. For a man accustomed to running his own show, few believed Perot would be happy with that arrangement.

The entrepreneurial Perot and the bureaucratic chairman of GM, Roger Smith: The two men clashed repeatedly.

"Perot believes in being a team player," an acquaintance of Perot was quoted in the January 5, 1987, issue of *Fortune*, "but he always wants to be the captain."

"The GM deal was a tremendous, marvelous financial deal that he [Perot] felt he had to do," said an associate to *Newsweek*. (January 9, 1989.) "He didn't realize how badly he would feel no longer being in charge of the company he had built over 20 years."

Perot and Smith were opposites, and their styles of running a business were so comparatively different—paramilitary versus bureaucratic—that many doubted the marriage of the two corporate moguls could last. Perot told *Financial World* (August 8–21, 1984) he thought differently. "They're missing the point. I work for all my customers. And Smith and I worked hard to structure this deal so that EDS will continue to run as it has." Perot didn't believe the differences were that great. He believed GM's method of employee selection, and training "is just like mine. It all goes back to perception versus reality. I'm perceived as speaking only to the birds. But in reality, I'm accountable to a lot of people."

The first responsibility for EDS was to improve GM's financial position with newly developed computers, but EDS also had the opportunity to market the integrated manufacturing systems it developed for GM. And it was believed EDS's data-processing strength could help channel GM into other business realms, such as finance, insurance, and health care.

"What we're trying to do," said EDS president Mort Meyerson to *Newsweek* (June 17, 1985), "is to make information available in the proper amount with the proper speed, to the proper people. Nobody has ever taken a mammoth corporation and done that before. It's going to happen everywhere. The question is, 'Who gets there first, and who does it best?'"

The opportunities excited Perot. In the same article in *Financial World,* he said he looked forward to the multi-billion dollar merger and the challenges it would create. "We will work with GM to build a worldwide state-of-the-art voice, data and video communications network."

Under the agreement, reported the Dallas *Morning News* (August 15, 1984), a new common stock—Class E—was issued. Shareholders of EDS stock could exchange it for the Class E common stock for $44 a share. Or they could exchange old EDS shares for $35.20 each plus securities. The new stock had one-half vote per share and one-half liquidation rights of GM common stock. GM issued 13,641,428 shares.

The two companies successfully worked out details to finalize the merger, and the Texas economy experienced almost instant benefits. EDS had to expand plans at its new facility in Plano, Texas, to accommodate the two companies' data processing operations. EDS announced plans to build a 90-acre data-processing facility onto its 2,640-acre Plano business park. Several months later, EDS announced the construction of another expansion project in Plano: a 32-story office skyscraper that, according to reports, would be the tallest building outside downtown Dallas. According to the Dallas *Morning News*, Perot was about to add 10,000 employees from GM onto the EDS payroll. Perot already had more than 14,500 employees of his own.

"You won't believe what they are doing up there," a source told the Dallas *Morning News*.

(March 28, 1985.) "It's not pie in the sky—it's happening right now."

While the computer mogul was occupied with the new GM deal and adding acreage to his business park, he was losing ground on a real estate deal just north of Plano.

The Dallas *Morning News* (March 28, 1985) reported that Perot made an offer to purchase 6,300 acres of land owned by Gulf National Land Corporation, a subsidiary of Gulf Broadcast Company, for $100 million. "They are in the negotiating process," reported an EDS spokesperson to the newspaper.

Earlier that year, Gulf Broadcast had announced that its board had agreed to liquidate the company and that it was selling its radio and television holdings. The company also said sales talks for its land holdings were being discussed, and Perot believed he was destined to become the next owner.

The next day, Gulf Broadcast said it had agreed to sell the land to Houston-based Gibraltar Savings & Loan Association, owned by First Texas Savings, for $130 million. Perot, who reported he already struck a deal with Gulf Broadcast for the land, was incensed.

Reported the February 20, 1985, Dallas *Morning News,* "If this is true, Gulf has sold it [the land] twice," a spokesperson for Perot quoted him as saying. However, Perot's was only a "handshake" deal. There had been no binding contract.

Perot, who historically never backs away from a brawl, put Gibraltar on notice that he was not giving in. "We have a deal, and they sold it twice. At this point, I thought I had seen everything," the Dallas *Morning News* reported Perot as saying. "They made another deal without telling us."

Gibraltar acquired the land for the development of homes, said J. Livingston Kosberg, a Houston businessman who owned the most interest in First Texas, in the Dallas *Morning News*.

"Our focus dealt with the larger piece— which, of course, is the most prominent piece," Kosberg told the Dallas *Morning News*. "I see a multi-use potential in the property—there can be as many as 25,000 to 30,000 homes built on the tract."

Gulf Broadcast ended up giving Perot an $8 million cash settlement for the "misunderstanding," but he still lost the land deal.

While Perot festered over the failed land deal, GM's Roger Smith was lining up high-priced corporations and experts to add to his conglomerate in hopes of building the perfect car. Perot looked upon most of these moves as a waste of energy and resources.

In 1985, GM finalized the purchase of Hughes Aircraft—an electronics, optical sensor, satellite, and missile contractor—for $5 billion. According to *U.S. News & World Report*, Smith

Perot addresses a press conference in July of 1988
concerning a business deal involving NCNB Corp.

hoped Hughes would give GM a distinct
advantage over auto makers building high-tech
cars.

Smith also entered into a joint venture with
a Japanese company building robots, contracted
for services with Britain's Group Lotus for their
expertise building engines and suspensions, and
merged five of his car divisions into two large
departments.

As 1986 drew to a close, reports started
pouring in about a series of business blunders
that cut GM's profits for the second year in a
row. These mistakes were expected to cause the
loss of tens of thousands of jobs, including

salaried and hourly workers, according to the
Dallas *Morning News.* (November 6, 1986.)

Though the mighty General Motors was
nearing worldwide revenues of more than $100
billion, its profit margins were steadily
dwindling and investors avoided the company's
common stock. GM loyalists watched as the
company's prominent position in the auto
industry slowly slipped. GM's financial
condition was dim. Executives announced
several plant closings and the scaling down of
some of their heavy spending projects.

Several factors contributed to GM's steady
decline in the industry. Labor costs—both blue-
collar and white-collar—were high, forcing
many layoffs. GM had a surplus of automobiles,
forcing costly sales incentives. The company
operated too many vehicle assembly and parts
manufacturing plants when sales were low.
Many said the car company lacked ingenuity in
creating sleek new styles. While its competitors
offered customers choices, GM produced too
many cars that looked alike.

Fed up with what he was seeing in his new
parent company, Perot blamed the men at the
top, announcing publicly that the responsibility
for making GM the leading car maker in the
world rests with top management.

"In business we want to blame middle
management, and we want to blame the people
in the factory. But those people don't . . . make
the policy," Perot said in the Dallas *Morning News*

December 8, 1986, edition. "They are totally at the mercy of the people who run the company."

Perot publicly aired his views on why GM continued its economic decline. "Right now at General Motors, the rules for success in the company have nothing to do with building the best car," Perot told the Washington *Post*. (January 14, 1990.) Top management is out of touch with the car business, he contended in the *Post*. GM was more concerned with providing top executives with chauffeured limousines and fat pay arrangements.

"If you're at the top of a car company, you don't learn much about your cars unless you drive them," said Perot in *Fortune*'s March 14, 1988, issue. "Anyone who needs a chauffeur to drive him to work is probably too old to be on the payroll."

Perot also berated GM leadership for giving themselves fat company bonuses during a period of crisis. In one instance, Roger Smith received a bonus of $930,000 on top of his $725,000 salary.

Smith's corporate difficulties and the way he handled them irked Perot, who was an "action man" not accustomed to getting himself tied up in bureaucratic red tape. Perot had his own way of doing things, and the man accustomed to running his own ball game was not about to sit quietly on the sidelines. GM was conservative and traditional, Perot wasn't. This was a definite obstacle that was difficult to overcome,

Ross Perot, Ross, Jr. (center), and Admiral William J.
Crowe (left) share a laugh in 1987.

and Perot didn't mind letting the public in on
the "closed door" corporate differences now
apparent at GM.

Perot voiced his opinion about many of the
company's decisions. He didn't like that GM
used Lotus to build engines when GM had
skilled engineers of its own. "You've got terrific
people at every level of GM," Perot told *U.S.
News & World Report.* (December 15, 1986.) "If
you could ever create an environment where
you tap their full potential, GM will carry the
day—it's all over for our competitors."

Perot carried his complaints even further,
targeting GM's stiff bureaucracy and decision-
making process. The problem wasn't with the
employees, Perot said, according to *U.S. News &*

World Report, who "are a lot better than the cars," it was with management. GM leadership could not make decisions. The GM army of commanders, said Perot to *U.S. News & World Report* (December 15, 1986), goes "ready, aim, aim, aim, aim. . . ." At EDS, "the first EDSer to see a snake kills it. At GM, first thing you do is organize a committee on snakes. Then, you bring in a consultant who knows a lot about snakes. Third thing, you talk about it for a year."

But Perot wasn't the only person talking to the press. Smith lashed back at Perot and his continual attacks. According to the Detroit *Free Press,* Smith said Perot was "not very familiar in total with our business" and that he was "very independent" and "impatient."

While Smith and other GM employees tired of Perot's constant heckling, others praised him for speaking out against the giant auto maker. In a poll conducted by *Ward's Auto World* magazine in 1986, about 96 percent of responding readers agreed with Perot's ideas for extreme change at GM.

"Ross Perot certainly has a better track record than GM's 14th floor at building a successful company," wrote EDS employee Eric Petersen to *Ward's Auto World.* R. L. Mowery of GM's Delco Products Division in Dayton, Ohio, said, "GM has been on a downward slide since upper-management people have come from finance-oriented areas. We need to return to . . .

people who know the difference between a nut and bolt and the dollar sign."

Smith and other top GM officials tried to silence Perot, but their efforts were in vain. Perot would not relent. He continued his public battle with his new bosses and lambasted Smith and everyone connected to the GM bureaucracy in various media nationwide.

The situation grew so bad that, according to the December 15, 1986, issue of *U.S. News & World Report,* top EDS executives tried to persuade American Telephone & Telegraph to buy part or all of EDS.

This was the last straw for Smith, and the "perfect" marriage of Perot's leadership and computer wizardry with GM's power and potential was at an end. According to *U.S. News & World Report,* when GM leaders learned of the subversive activities of the EDS executives, Perot and three top EDS executives, including Mort Meyerson, were asked to relinquish not only all ties to the company but all stock holdings. GM bought back the 12 million GM Class E shares the four men owned, Perot himself netting some $750 million.

As reported in the February 2, 1986, edition of the Dallas *Morning News,* in the statement announcing Perot's split from GM, Smith stated, "The strength of our relationship has been that we have approached our common business problems in different ways, using the perspectives of different backgrounds.

"We have always agreed on the primary goal: to be the leader in our industry and the most technologically advanced company in the world."

The settlement agreement also included a gag order on both Perot and Smith. Should Perot or Smith publicly criticize the other, the offender would face fines of up to $7.5 million.

The settlement also included a clause forbidding Perot from starting a for-profit company before the end of 1989. He could, however, start a business anytime after June 1, 1988, provided it didn't turn a profit.

But Perot swore he would not abandon ship. Although agreeing to the terms of the settlement, he placed the money in an escrow account and offered GM until December 15, 1986, to reconsider.

"I want to give them the chance to do the right thing," Perot told the Dallas *Morning News*. (December 8, 1986.)

The GM board unanimously reaffirmed its decision that same day and appointed Lester M. Alberthal, Jr., to succeed Perot as EDS president.

Perot felt it was still important to use EDS to help make GM the most powerful auto maker in the industry. "Where I fit in is not important," Perot said in the Dallas *Morning News*. (December 8, 1986.) "The strength of both companies is what is important here."

Perot, who believes ardently in his missions, appeared on ABC's *Business World* television

Perot and his only son, Ross, Jr., in 1989.

show. Despite a possible $7.5 million fine
should he criticize GM, he opened fire on Smith
and GM.

On December 7, 1986, the Dallas *Morning
News* quoted Perot from the show: "I just don't
want to be a part of an organization that's
closing plants, laying people off. I want to be
part of an organization that's growing,
dynamic and creating jobs," Perot said.

In the *Business World* interview, Perot
denied any interest in replacing Smith as GM
chairman. "No, no, no, no, no, no. I never had

any desire to have a management role in GM."
He only wanted GM to reach its full potential.

"When you're the biggest car maker in the
world, selling more cars than anybody else but
not making much money, when you've got
more in the way of financial resources, more
human talent than anyone else, then it's
absolutely inexcusable that you are not the best
across the board."

Wall Street did not respond well to Perot's
selling out. On judgment day, GM's common
and Class E stock were among the most actively
traded shares on the New York Stock Exchange.
In one day, more than 2 million shares changed
hands, and GM closed at 71½, down 1⅜. Class
E had nearly 1.6 million shares traded, closing
at 26⅞, down 4½. Both GM common stock and
Class E stock lost more than $800 million in
market value the day Perot split from EDS and
General Motors.

Under the contract, Perot was to receive $60
per share for his Class E stock, a 123 percent
premium the day he split from GM. That didn't
help other shareholders.

"The difficulty first and foremost is that GM
has made an offer to senior management to
take them out at $60 a share, when the stock
was $31 in the morning," David Readerman, an
analyst at Smith Barney in New York, told the
Dallas *Morning News.* (December 2, 1986.)
"What happens to the remaining shareholders?
It's not a fair deal for everyone else who took

GM's good faith commitment that it would maximize their investment."

The United Auto Workers (UAW) union was also displeased about the breakup. The buy-out was "the wrong thing to do. It gives the wrong impression to the whole world," said UAW president Owen Bieber to the Dallas *Morning News*. (December 7, 1986.) "You're talking about one-and-a-half times the savings [GM expects] in closing 11 plants."

A group of investors expressed their opposition by filing a shareholders resolution with GM condemning the buy-out. The investors, led by Wisconsin Investment Board, hoped to prevent similar situations in the future.

Despite the ill will between Perot and GM, Perot stated at a Dallas news conference that he would remain with EDS as an essential component to the company. He failed to explain specifics. The announcement came on the day he and GM separated.

"I will stay here at EDS, and I will continue to work with EDS people doing all the things I have been doing."

He stated that EDS was involved in several large projects and that "it would be a serious mistake for anything to occur that takes us out."

In the days following the announcement, Perot continued to stress his support for EDS and the auto industry's line workers. He also expressed his loyalty toward EDS employees.

"I will be here as long as they want," he told the Dallas *Morning News*. (December 2, 1986.) "I feel a tremendous obligation to our people to provide them security in case anything goes wrong." He pledged that EDS's headquarters would remain in Dallas and that its employees would not have to decide between unemployment and leaving Texas for Detroit.

The split between Perot and GM was a major headline maker for some time. It had a wide impact and piqued the interest of more than a few people. And most people, from analysts to assembly line workers, had an opinion.

Commenting on Perot's divorce from GM, Bernard Addo, an analyst at Argus Research Corp., told the Dallas *Morning News* (December 2, 1986), "It appeared that although Perot tried to point out to GM what it should and should not do, he went about it by going out of his way to criticize the company.

"It was a clash of two men with extraordinary strong wills. There was Roger Smith, the epitome of corporate culture and a team player, and Ross Perot, the epitome of entrepreneurial spirit," Addo continued. "Somehow, they just couldn't fit together on the same team. Perot meant well, but the way he went about it came across as management bashing."

Lester Alberthal, new CEO for EDS, was interviewed by the Dallas *Morning News*.

Ross Perot has been involved with more than just EDS. He
has also had a hand in several real estate deals.

(December 5, 1986.) "I think most of the deep
scars were in the area of the four people who
left," said Alberthal. "The day-to-day
relationship is better. It does not mean that
everything is rosy, but we were trying to
accomplish massive change."

Employees at GM's Arlington plant stated
their opinions on the Perot-Smith controversy.

"I think it [the controversy] is the best thing
that's ever happened to us," said Don
Hildebrand, a monitor on the assembly line, to
the Dallas *Morning News.* (December 2, 1986.)
Perot "doesn't think he's too big to walk down
on the shop floor and talk to the working
people. . . . I think it's the big shots up there are
afraid he's going to get too much power."

Pete Peterson, chairman of the bargaining committee for UAW, believed Perot cared about his employees and how they were treated.

"I feel he has a lot of sympathy for good, honest, working people," Peterson said in the Dallas *Morning News.* (December 8, 1986.) "What Mr. Perot has been saying is an echo of what we've been saying."

Unlike other top executives who visited the plants, Peterson said Perot always took time to listen to blue-collar needs and complaints.

"Perot went out there with me. He didn't go with an entourage. We didn't have a planned tour, cleaning up the path we were going to take. . . . We had beans and cornbread with the guys on the line." Peterson said Perot answered all their question specifically. "It was a real boost."

But not all employees appreciated Perot's attempts at change, according to the Dallas *Morning News.* (December 8, 1986.)

"I don't think it's his affair," said Jim Fisk, a data communications employee. "He should do it [bring change] within the system."

Other employees expressed anger toward Perot and the merger with GM.

"They brought in better equipment," said an anonymous source to the Dallas *Morning News.* (December 8, 1986.) "But they didn't know what to do with it. . . . I can't tell you how many screwups there were because they didn't know whether they were coming or going."

Perot speaks with the press in Washington, D.C., shortly after GM bought out his interest in GM.

A common question was what sweeping changes Perot would make at GM if he had the opportunity. Perot outlined some of his thoughts in the February 15, 1988, issue of *Fortune*. He said that although many GM employees were indoctrinated in the personnel philosophy of GM-Saturn (GM's new division), talking about that philosophy would not produce results.

"The key ingredient," he said, "is to put these ideas into practice throughout GM—execute, execute, execute!"

Perot in his office in 1987 with his son and one of his four daughters.

Perot said GM needs to call its top officials together and announce that the company has more talent, money, research capability, and manufacturing facilities than any other car maker. With these facts in mind, said Perot, it should logically follow that GM is first at building the best cars in the world.

"It is not," said Perot. "GM has failed to tap the full potential of its resources, especially its people. This must be changed."

GM must understand that it "is playing all day every day in an economic superbowl. It is a harsh game—the losers lose their jobs and their companies. . . . GM can win and keep its people at work only by being the best—by building the best cars in the world."

Ross, Jr., is handling the Fort Worth Alliance Airport project—the model of which is in the foreground—for his father.

Perot said further that the "UAW must recognize that they can build the finest cars in the world only by working closely together. With 800,000 jobs at stake, GM must win."

For GM to build the best cars worldwide, said Perot, the company must listen to its customers, dealers, factory-workers, and designers. "Their ideas, fresh from the marketplace," said Perot, "will make GM the best in the world."

In *The New York Times* March 20, 1992, issue, Perot criticized corporate executives for awarding themselves "obscene salaries" while ignoring the needs of its employees and shareholders. Perot told the *Times* he had the same annual salary, $68,000, when he left GM in 1986 as he had in the 1960s. But Perot's statement did not go without criticism.

"If I owned 100 percent of the stock, I'd love to keep my salary low, too, because that means my second-in-command doesn't get as much and my third-in-command doesn't get as much," said Donald C. Clark of Household International, Inc.

Fortune (February 15, 1988) gave Roger Smith an opportunity to rebut Perot.

When Perot said GM was incapable of making decisions, Smith responded, "We make decisions every minute of every day. We use our committee structure to review decisions, not to make them."

Perot spoke out when GM officials awarded themselves hefty bonuses in 1986 without granting any to their employees. Smith argued that General Motors had a negotiated profit-sharing plan with UAW that was added on to an employee's base salary if company profits reached a certain quota. "For managers GM has had a bonus plan since 1918," Smith said. "The GM philosophy has been a relatively low salary and high performance bonus; if you took comparable levels at Ford and Chrysler, our base salaries were always lower because we had more at risk."

When Perot accused GM of not tapping the full potential of its resources, Smith stated that it "might have been true some years ago, but

Ross Perot and his wife, Margot, in 1987. It was her
$1,000 that first staked EDS in 1962.

we have made great strides—a tremendous
turnaround in product quality, in our plants, in
turning people around."

Despite Smith's defenses, Perot's attacks
continued. For years after leaving General
Motors, Perot openly berated GM's
management.

After Perot left GM, many people wondered
what the corporate billionaire was going to do
with the $750 million he had placed in escrow.
But Perot, who has become a legend using his
immense wealth for the good of others, told the
Dallas *Morning News* (December 2, 1986) that he

planned to spend it on the American
people.

"My plan is to use the money in venture
capital to create jobs. . . . I would use this to
create good, stable jobs."

Perot believed the responsibility of creating
jobs in this country falls jointly on the shoulders
of the government and large corporations. He
preached this whenever given the opportunity.
Perot stressed that strong, prosperous companies
were vital to the American people and
government. He said America needs growing
businesses because it needs more taxpayers,
which is fundamental to the economic strength
of this country.

When government and corporate America
are successful in putting people back to work,
Perot believed the country would see a ripple
effect. Not only would those workers bring home
a paycheck and pay taxes but the government
would no longer have to support them through
costly welfare programs.

Perot also thought it was incumbent on
America as a whole to foster working
environments that encourage the development
of bright minds and fresh ideas. Perot's next
major investment demonstrated that belief.
Perot invested his money toward super-
computers developed for universities.

While sitting at home flipping through
television channels, Perot chanced to see Steven
Jobs, co-founder of Apple Computer,

Perot enjoys some relaxing moments on a Texas lake in 1989. His billions have bought him independence.

brainstorming with colleagues on the screen before him. They were discussing their new company, Next, which was developing computers designed specifically for universities.

According to the February 7, 1987, issue of *Newsweek,* the highly sophisticated programs could provide simulations for DNA research, for example, or they could teach nonmusicians about composition.

"Computers," Perot said in *Newsweek*, "are the closet thing to a one-on-one tutor situation."

Though Next was a year away from shipping its first product, Perot wanted in on the deal. "I've never seen a group of people so focused on being the best at what they do. They're absolutely eaten up with it."

Perot never underestimated the power of education and its importance in a free America. "If you make a great product for higher education, you've probably made an incredible product for the business market," Perot told *Business Week.* (October 24, 1988.)

Perot contacted Jobs the next day to explain his interest, and Jobs listened carefully. "The thing that impressed me most about Ross," Jobs said in the Dallas *Morning News* (January 31, 1987), "was that, while most people focus on the bottom line—which he certainly did—what Ross looked at first is what I call the 'top-line'—which is the people and the strategy."

For $20 million dollars, or 16 percent of the company's stock, Perot bought into a company with an estimated value of $126 million even before there was a product.

By this time, the agreement with GM was nearing expiration; Perot was ready. The day the contract expired, he announced he was back in business with a newly formed company, Perot Systems Corporation.

The business, funded by a partnership made up of the Perot family, could not yet compete for profit due to the GM buy-out agreement, but it could compete for cost. Perot announced he was prepared to sign a large contract with the U.S. Postal Service to examine ways to cut costs and increase efficiency. The contract, at least for the time being, would only cover expenses.

His work on behalf of POWs and MIAs has earned Perot several humanitarian awards and honors.

The EDS response to Perot's announcement was reported in the June 2, 1988, Dallas *Morning News.* "He started a new company and industry 25 years ago. We are disappointed that he would choose to compete against the company he founded and its employees . . . but we welcome competition from any quarter . . . we are a strong team, experienced and deep in talent."

Perot claimed he intended to operate a one-man company at Perot Systems and would not be hiring. However, he left the door open should someone of quality feel the need to join his quest. "I really don't want anybody to join this company, unless they can't stand not to be a part of it," he told the Dallas *Morning News.* (June 2, 1988.)

Within a week, eight middle-level EDS executives announced they were leaving the company and signing on with their old boss. The Dallas *Morning News* (June 2, 1988) reported Perot's proud announcement that he had gathered together "the top guns of the computer industry, the fighting generals with mud on their boots and dirt on their uniforms . . . guys who like to climb cliffs with ice on 'em."

Within hours after Perot's announcement, GM's Class E stock dropped 2¾ points. The sudden departure of important employees created uncertainty about the company's future strength. EDS refused to take Perot's move in stride. His old company immediately filed a lawsuit claiming Perot breached an agreement barring him from competing with his former company until the end of the next year. The Dallas *Morning News* (September 28, 1988) reported that Perot responded by claiming "it is a reaction to the test of direct competition with Perot Systems."

Perot was optimistic he would never see the inside of a courtroom. And he filed a countersuit against EDS accusing them of trying to put his new computer services firm out of business.

Perot's battle with EDS was only one of his concerns. There also was controversy brewing over his new contract with the U.S. Postal Service.

Postmaster General Anthony Frank (background) and
Ross Perot signed an ill-fated contract in 1988.

Perot Systems signed a $500,000 contract to
study cost savings in the $36 billion postal
system. The early portion of the contract was for
costs only, but after Perot Systems could legally
turn a profit, the company was promised as
much as ten percent of the savings it cut from
the postal budget.

Things looked fine until the General
Accounting Office told Senate aides that it
objected to the exclusive nature of Perot's
contract with the Postal Service. The contract

never went out for bid, as most government projects did. The General Services Administration declared Perot's consulting contract with the Postal Service illegal and void.

Attorneys for Perot and the Postal Service argued in the U.S. Court of Appeals that a government contract review board had no authority to find their no-bid consulting contract illegal. The Court of Appeals agreed and ruled the no-bid contract with the mail carrier did not violate federal statutes, clearing the way for Perot to resume his consulting work.

However, Postmaster General Anthony Frank soon announced the cancellation of the contract. Frank said the lengthy suspension of work crippled efforts to accomplish his goal.

Perot took the news well. "We understand and agree with the decision made by the postmaster general," said Perot in the Dallas *Morning News.* (December 17, 1988.) The Postal Service "can and must be modernized using the latest technology to provide better service at the lowest possible cost."

Although the feud between GM and Perot as well as the Postal Service episode are well known, not all of Perot's business ventures are so controversial. In one of his most fascinating real estate ventures, the Dallas *Morning News* (October 6, 1988) reported that Perot announced he wanted to use Fort Worth Alliance Airport— the centerpiece of a planned industrial airport— to create a "spaceport."

Perot—a strong supporter of family values—believes the
family is the cornerstone of American society.

Perot had spent years accumulating land in
a wide open area in order to master this plan.
According to the December 1988 *Texas
Monthly*, giant cargo jets would land and taxi
up to high-tech factories lining the runways.
This would allow the aircraft to unload their

contents directly onto assembly lines for manufacturing and then load the finished products back onto the planes for distribution.

According to the *Texas Monthly* article, workers would live in Perot's vision of America's future. Perot intended to build small communities complete with shopping and schools around the spaceport. Perot the family man touted the innovative airport community as more than just a method of efficiency: Workers would be able to go home to have lunch with their children.

A Federal Aviation Administration (FAA) official, however, told *Texas Monthly* that Perot's plans were too "far-fetched to even speculate about at this point." The FAA hadn't even designed criteria by which such spaceports would be built.

From his youth at IBM to his rise to billionaire, Ross Perot has shown perseverance and hard work, setting high standards and demanding much sacrifice from those around him. Perot's tenacity is greatly responsible for his success. Many of his business dealings have become the stuff of legend: His start-up of EDS with only $1,000 to his public jousting with General Motors. Even today, Perot continues to be a controversial and powerful personality. In the world of business, he is a man of action. The question for the public to decide is: How will Ross Perot's business methods translate to the political realm?

CHAPTER 3

PEROT: MAN AS LEGEND

"I have always felt strongly about standing up for what I believe. And maybe that's what [succeeding] is all about."—Ross Perot
Dallas Morning News; September 6, 1985

Opposite: Ross Perot chats with a Laotian child in April 1970, shortly after arriving in Laos on a mission to determine the status of U.S. prisoners of war.

Ross Perot may not believe in legends. Indeed, he has often referred to himself as a myth rather than as a legend. But his reputation as a businessman and his rapid rise to great wealth brought him almost instant legendary status.

In a December 1, 1980, *Newsweek* interview Perot remarked, "I don't think I am any different from most Americans, except that I have a great deal of independence. I have the time and funds to do what I do."

But his colorful career, from the early days as an IBM salesman extraordinaire to his campaign for MIAs in Vietnam to his involuntary "grass roots" draft into presidential politics, only served to perpetuate his image.

The press hailed him as the "welfare billionaire" who ran Electronic Data Systems with the militaristic control and efficiency of a boot camp. He made a point to hire Vietnam War veterans whenever possible and enlisted all new employees in rigorous training programs that lasted for months.

Any and all employees of Perot were subject to stringent codes of conduct, both in and out of the office. Rules and restrictions governed everything from fashion and facial hair guidelines to rules against extramarital affairs. All aspects of an employee's life were covered. In the employee cafeteria where Perot ate with all the other workers, he was referred to as Ross.

When long and demanding hours mandated by Perot kept husbands away from home, Perot would attempt to make amends to wives with gifts of flowers and even shares of EDS stock.

Throughout, his goal was increased productivity and ultimate success. From the beginning, Perot had resolved to create not just a corporation, but a culture, wrote Peter Elkind in the December 1988 issue of *Texas Monthly*.

"I want people who are smart, tough, self-reliant, have a history of success since childhood, a history of being the best at what they've done, people who love to win," Perot told Elkind. "And if you run out of people who love to win, look for people who hate to lose."

Even Perot's harshest critics are hard put to deny his salesmanship and uncanny ability to lead—attributes that have contributed greatly to not only his fortune but also his exciting reputation.

Ironically, perhaps, Perot gained much of his fame and mystique outside the realm of high finance. His celebrity status was directly related to a deep-rooted love for his country, which earned him the title "Superpatriot."

As reported by the April 1983 issue of the *Saturday Evening Post*, Perot maintains that "It is important for people to have this feeling so that they can continue to enjoy living in a self-governing country where people can make changes to fit the current need."

In 1969 (above), Perot supported Nixon's Vietnam policy.
A decade later, Perot fought his own "war" in Iran.

The depth of Perot's patriotism and his sense
of responsibility to his employees is amply
illustrated by his instrumental role in the daring
1979 rescue of two EDS employees from a
fortress-like prison in Iran.

The story begins in the waning days of 1978, a tense period in international relations. EDS was under a $41 million contract with Iran to computerize social security and national health care records. The arrangement might have been straightforward enough under normal circumstances, but Iran was a nation engulfed in violent change at the time. The power of Shah Mohammed Reza Pahlevi was visibly slipping as massive public demonstrations demanded the return of the exiled Ayatollah Ruhollah Khomeini. On December 16, the day that EDS's contract with Iran was scheduled to expire, the Shah seized the passports of EDS workers Paul Chiapparone and William Gaylord.

As reported in the February 26, 1979, edition of *The New York Times*, on December 28, 1978, the Shah ordered both of the Americans jailed. Perot was outraged, saying that his employees were being held "hostage" to ensure EDS would return to start up the new computer systems following Iran's general strike. Perot was commanded to pay $12.75 million in ransom for the safe release of his men.

A ransom payment would have been a reasonably neat way to handle the matter. However, the entire Iranian banking system had broken down in the midst of the nation's civil unrest, and Perot claimed it was impossible to manage a transfer of the funds. He needed help fast, so his next step was to contact the United States government.

"We repeatedly sought help from the State Department, the Defense Department, the White House and every level of our government," Perot said in a press conference. But because help could not be found, he decided to take on the task himself.

Perot went inside his own company, EDS, to recruit a team of 15 commandos, all wartime veterans. He then enlisted the help of adventurer Arthur "Bull" Simons. With Simons at the helm and Perot making use of his vast wealth, the team began an intense period of training at an undisclosed site near Dallas. The Los Angeles *Times* reported that, by mid-January of 1979, Simons had traveled with part of the team to Teheran, Iran. The group spent the next three weeks in hiding, living a clandestine existence in a volatile, unfriendly nation.

According to the April 1983 issue of the *Saturday Evening Post*, Perot utilized a forged passport to arrive in Teheran about the same time as Simons. Perot was ready for action but realized a new plan was called for after getting a look at the imposing Gasre fortress that held his employees; he knew it would be impossible for a unit as small as his to overcome the prison by force.

Later, armed with a revised agenda, Perot ventured into the crowded streets and returned to the prison. By luck, he arrived at the same time an American State Department official was checking on the condition of the EDS hostages, the *Post* reported. Perot was mistaken for a U.S. diplomat and allowed to enter the prison. He alerted Chiapparone and Gaylord that a staged prison riot would erupt in a matter of days, and that they should use it as an opportunity to escape. They were told to make their way to a waiting car that would spirit them to safety in Turkey.

Perot gave an unspecified amount of money to a group of Iranian anti-Shah revolutionaries and instructed them to prepare to start a riot outside of the prison. While stationed in Istanbul on February 11, Perot ordered the riot to commence. As described by Perot to *The New York Times*, Gaylord and Chiapparone "climbed the walls and fled through intense gunfire for about two miles on foot" before walking and hitchhiking ten miles to rendezvous with Simons and a portion of the team. The rest of the squad was just across the Turkish border ready to fly into Iran to make the rescue if necessary.

The action was not necessary and Perot, along with Gaylord and Chiapparone, Simons, and the other 15 EDS employees headed to Dallas for a hero's welcome.

The New York Times quoted Perot as saying, "We were successful in our efforts to arrange with revolutionary leaders in the areas to have the prison stormed by an Iranian mob."

Nevertheless, there is some question about the accuracy of Perot's account of the daring escape and the events leading up to it. At the time of the incident, the U.S. government confirmed reports of the Shah's arrest of the EDS employees, but the arrests were apparently in conjunction with an investigation of Iranian ministers involved in possible corruption charges related to the awarding of contracts to American business concerns. *The New York Times* said the $12.75 million actually was the amount of money owed to the Iranian government by EDS for services not rendered.

Other possible glitches in Perot's adventure story are found in conflicting reports from interviews with Simons and Perot. And the *Times* report noted Gasre was just one of many prisons, police stations, and jails stormed that day by armed revolutionaries celebrating the return from exile of the Ayatollah. The goal was freedom for terrorists and political prisoners locked away by the Shah.

And one writer noted that if the riot was staged by Perot, he not only violated the law but turned more than just the "innocent" EDS employees loose.

"The mission's shining success made its critics sound churlish," Peter Elkind wrote in the *Texas Monthly*. "But to free the jailed EDS pair, Perot's commandos orchestrated a riot that sprang 11,000 political prisoners and criminals—including murderers and rapists—

from a Teheran prison. In the process, the mission violated U.S. and international law."

Over time, the rescue has assumed a legendary status, thanks largely to author Ken Follett's book, *On Wings of Eagles*, which was later dramatized as a popular network-TV miniseries.

Actor Richard Crenna played Perot in *On Wings of Eagles*, a TV miniseries dramatizing the Iran rescue mission.

The jailbreak did not end Perot's
involvement in Iranian affairs. When Khomeini
followers stormed the American embassy in
Teheran in November 1979 and American lives
were at stake, Perot was summoned. As reported
in the April 1983 *Saturday Evening Post*, Perot
said, "Our team was asked to consult with the
federal government. . . . But we had a strong
difference of opinion with some of the military
and with White House staffers. There was a lack
of direction and go-go spirit at the White House.
And [President] Carter was so indecisive. In a
situation like that, you put the right crew
together and let them go."

And when Carter's botched 1980 rescue
attempt left some Americans dead and others
stranded in the desert, Perot said his men were
at the ready: "The same people who went with
us to Iran," he told the *Post*, "came to me at
8:30 A.M. that morning and volunteered to go
back if they could rescue those left in the
desert."

The Iranian situations did not mark Ross
Perot's first foray into international politics.
While he was thrust involuntarily into the
hostage crisis, his commitment to American
soldiers believed still alive in Vietnamese prison
camps was a purposeful one that evolved from
his deep love for his country.

The first of many POW-related efforts by
Perot was the much-heralded 1969 Christmas

At a Bangkok news conference in 1969, Perot announced his plan to air-drop Christmas presents to U.S. POWs.

drop. While the patriotic Texan probably would have made the effort on his own accord, it later was revealed he was working under orders from President Nixon. Perot's goal was to deliver Christmas presents to every captive American soldier in Vietnam. Perot said Nixon encouraged the scheme to discredit the North Vietnamese and to counter antiwar activists.

Alexander Haig, at that time deputy to National Security Advisor Henry Kissinger, and liaison between Perot and the Nixon administration, was quoted in the April 27, 1992, *New York Times* as saying, "I would not say we formally asked [Perot] to do it as such. But we endorsed the concept."

Perot "vividly remembered" a different conversation, and he told it to the Dallas *Morning News* for the June 29, 1986, edition: "He [Kissinger] said, 'Look, the prisoners are dying from torture and neglect. We're going to Vietnamize the war, but it's going to take three years. Half the men are going to die. We want you to take your own money and embarrass the North Vietnamese into changing the treatment.'

"But I couldn't say I was doing this at the request of the government," Perot added.

Perot's Christmas-present plan stalled when North Vietnamese leaders said they could not allow the gesture as long as American planes were destroying their country. Undeterred from the plan's general idea, Perot devised a scheme to fly to Moscow and use its postal service to mail gifts to the American POWs in North Vietnam. Armed with an adequate supply of reporters, mail, medicine, and Christmas dinners, Perot chartered two 707 airliners and headed out. However, the governments in Moscow and North Vietnam rejected Perot and sent him home, still armed with his bundles and a $4 million tab.

One newspaper headline called Perot the "Lone Star Santa Claus"; some reports claimed he was being laughed at and ridiculed. He was not fazed by criticism. While admitting partial defeat, he said it was just that—partial. His efforts did lead to better treatment of American prisoners, he said.

When North Vietnam refused a Christmas 1969 air drop
of holiday gifts to U.S. POWs, Perot repackaged presents,
intending to mail them from Moscow.

A September 4, 1986, piece in the Dallas
Morning News gave Perot an opportunity to
clarify his motives. "I never cared if the public
thought I was a funny guy trying to deliver
Christmas presents," he said. "It was just a tactic
to embarrass the North Vietnamese into
changing treatment of the prisoners, which they
did."

Still hopeful of providing a Christmas to American POWs, Perot met the media on one of his specially chartered jets in the waning days of 1969.

In the long run, the failed plan set a precedent by which the U.S. government continued to bankroll covert operations through the largess of wealthy supporters in the private sector. The Christmas drop proved to be only the first of many "favors" Perot did for his country.

In 1970, not even a full year after the Christmas plan, Perot was back on track aiming for, if nothing else, better treatment of American POWs and MIAs. This time his ammunition included public appearances by the unhappy wives of five American soldiers either missing or locked away in a jungle camp somewhere in North Vietnam. *Newsweek* said Perot was trying to "soften" enemy attitudes toward captured Americans.

Molly Ivins, a columnist for the Fort Worth *Star-Telegram* and a combination admirer and antagonist of Perot, referred to his crusade to free Americans overseas as "Tell It to Hanoi!" Driven by fierce patriotism, this was Perot's way of rallying America behind the estimated 1,600 U.S. servicemen imprisoned in North Vietnam.

Ivins related the story of Perot's crusade in the May 4, 1992, issue of *Time*: "Perot brought his 'Tell It to Hanoi!' campaign to the Texas state capitol in 1971 on what may still be the single weirdest day in the history of that peculiar institution. Jets roared over Austin in 'missing man' formation, while beneath the rotunda, in hour after hour of bloodstained oratory, brows were darkened and teeth gnashed over the fate of Our Boys. It was a patriotic orgy."

The same issue of *Time* gave Perot a forum from which to pose a rhetorical question: "Is there any question what our grandfathers and great-grandfathers would have done for 1,600 men held prisoner only a day's ride from Austin?" Perot made his point clearer by adding that, thanks to the technology available in 1970, Hanoi was only 24 hours away by plane.

Perot's involvement with the POW and MIA saga extended far beyond the waning years of the Vietnam War and into the Reagan era. During the latter period he privately funded reconnaissance missions into Laos and sponsored his own trips to Vietnam to meet with government officials and urge the release of Americans. In 1985 Perot volunteered to serve as chairman of a commission made up of retired military personnel and former POWs to carry out Reagan's call for public awareness of the MIA issue. According to reports at the time, 164 Texans were among the Vietnam veterans who never returned from the war and were never officially counted among the dead.

Perot, well known for doling out great sums of money for causes he considers worthy, offered $4.2 million in 1986 for a rumored videotape that allegedly contained absolute proof that American POWs were living in Laos. That tape could have validated at least some of the 136 of 881 sightings of American prisoners in Southeast Asia, sightings that currently remain under investigation by the Defense Department.

"I was asked by our government to pursue this thing, to get the tape if it existed," Perot was quoted by the Associated Press. "I said fine, it's a long shot, but I'll be glad to do it."

Perot's concern for American POWs became a quest to locate MIAs once the Vietnam War ended.

Perot's generous offer had no takers, which led most observers to believe the tape did not exist and the whole thing had been a hoax.

Just months later a request from Reagan to investigate the MIA situation and possible solutions went sour for the government. At the time, Richard L. Armitage, assistant secretary of defense, was the key U.S. official working to identify and free American MIAs. But it was reported that President and Nancy Reagan suspected that the search for American POWs was being mishandled.

Perot, assisted by several aides touring Washington undercover, allegedly uncovered information linking Richard Armitage to a narcotics and weapons-smuggling scam that had been based in Southeast Asia in the early 1970s. Perot also charged that Armitage currently was associated with a Vietnamese woman, Nguyet O'Rourke, who had been linked to organized crime figures in this country.

Perot feared Armitage's relationship with O'Rourke, one that the woman admitted dated back to Saigon and involved socializing and drinking at her home in a Washington suburb. As reported by the Dallas *Morning News* on February 2, 1987, Perot felt that the situation could adversely affect important negotiations with Vietnam. He uncovered a copy of a letter written on Defense Department stationery urging a Virginia court to "show mercy" to

O'Rourke after her arrest for running an illicit $50,000-a-week gambling operation in the Washington suburbs. The evidence suggested that she was not the ideal companion for Armitage.

Perot took his charges to Vice President Bush. Bush said he did not have jurisdiction and steered Perot to the appropriate authorities. Perot would not quit, even after National Security Advisor Frank Carlucci asked him to back off from the investigation. According to the Dallas *Morning News* story, Carlucci said Armitage was too valuable to the Pentagon.

In 1970, Perot offered to "build facilities" for the people of North Vietnam in exchange for release of U.S. POWs.

Perot would not comment on the situation publicly, saying only that his work for Reagan was classified. The only official word from the Defense Department was that the arms and drugs allegations were old and unfounded and no investigation was pending.

Following this peculiar turn of events, Perot continued to press his efforts on behalf of American MIAs. The next time his name surfaced in connection with Vietnam was months later, when he traveled there on his own accord for three days of secret meetings.

Perot received great public acclaim for his daring and adventurous rescue of EDS employees from Iran and for his unending support of American servicemen missing in Southeast Asia. However, one cause he did not receive credit for at the time was his attempted rescue of other American hostages hidden away in the tumultuous Middle East. More than a year passed before the public knew Perot willingly handed over more than $2 million to representatives of the U.S. government for hostage buys. Perot's gesture was kept secret because it might have been part of the clandestine Iran-Contra affair. And when news finally reached the public, it wasn't entirely clear whether the money Perot gave to Lt. Colonel Oliver North was intended to free hostages or to fund Nicaraguan rebels.

Perot was quoted in the Dallas *Morning News* on December 14, 1986, as saying he

Top and above: Perot was being pragmatic when he visited North Vietnamese POWs in South Vietnam in 1970. He hoped the gesture would aid U.S. POWs.

"never put a penny into any kind of Contra effort, directly or indirectly. Ollie [North] never asked me."

Perot continued this theme in the June 20, 1988, *U.S. News & World Report*, where he said, "I told [North] it was a dumb idea. I am not going to get involved in wars that aren't supported by the American people."

Perot's initial involvement in the hostage plan began with the rescue of Brigadier General James Dozier, who had been kidnapped in Italy in 1981 and held by Red Brigade terrorists. Perot said he was wakened by a 2 A.M. call from a senior Pentagon official who asked for $500,000 to secure Dozier's release. The money was immediately wired to an Italian bank. Dozier was later released and the money returned.

Perot's quick response in the Dozier crisis showed the United States government it had someone it could count on.

Perot was "the choice of first resort for covert ops. He got things done quickly, unlike the CIA," a former National Security Council official told *U.S. News*.

"I've been doing this since 1969, trying to help Americans in distress around the world," Perot told the Dallas *Morning News*, December 2, 1986. He added he firmly believes it is the government's sworn duty to help Americans in distress overseas. However, as he understands the government policy, officials will not use tax dollars. Instead, they will seek out interested

Perot's activism has brought him such awards as the
Defense Department Award for Distinguished Service.

citizens and solicit their help. As far as Perot is
concerned, to answer solicitations of this sort is
his duty.

"It's a thankless job," Perot told *U.S. News*,
"but it's the right thing to do. If the shoe were
on the other foot and I was over there, I'd sure
want someone to help me."

When CIA station chief William Buckley
and several others were taken hostage in
Lebanon in 1985, Perot was among the first to
receive a phone call from Oliver North.

"North told me that we had to find out what
Buckley told the Iranians," Perot said.

Several different accounts of the attempted trade for Buckley were published. *Time* reported on June 8, 1987, that two federal drug enforcement agents contacted an informant who arranged a deal to have the hostages released for $200,000. When the CIA refused to dole out the money without proof it was dealing with Buckley's captors, North turned to Perot. Although the agents warned it appeared to be a scam, North, desperate to find Buckley, turned over the money. It disappeared.

In October 1985, Buckley's captors announced his execution. Still, North convinced Perot to part with another $100,000. The money was never seen again. The final attempt involved Perot sending $2 million (according to the Washington *Post*; $1 million according to *Time* magazine) via courier to Cyprus, where an exchange for five hostages would take place. After a week of waiting, the courier returned home with the money. National Security Advisor Robert McFarlane claimed North told him Perot was upset about North not keeping him informed during the mission, which eventually culminated in the loss of $500,000.

Referring to the lost money, Perot said, "I would rather try and fail than not try."

When the Iran-Contra affair became public and Perot's name surfaced, he admitted to donating money to help free American hostages. However, regardless of confusing statements given by North and others, he vehemently denied any knowledge of his money going to buy arms or going to the Contras.

"The thing that I find fascinating is that if any of these congressmen had questions, why didn't they call me. . . . These turkeys will hear from me tomorrow. This is really unprofessional. . . . There's a lot of fantasy here," Perot said.

But even when the heat of the arms sale scandal was on, Perot could look back on a successful mission that resulted in the "escape" of Jeremy Levin, the Beirut bureau chief of Cable News Network, who was being held in the Middle East.

At the request of the U.S. government, Perot enlisted the aid of the Rev. Jesse Jackson, the one man who successfully negotiated the release of a hostage in the Middle East (Navy flier Robert Goodman in December 1983).

There is some question whether Jackson was actually sent to encourage the release of Levin or Buckley. However, in January 1985 Jackson traveled to Europe accompanied by his staff, family, and an associate of Perot, who covered all expenses. When Jackson returned he told Perot one American hostage would soon be free. Perot was impressed when, just days later, Jeremy Levin escaped his captors.

In stories in the December 4, 1986, and May 3, 1988, Dallas *Morning News*, Perot noted that

"Jesse Jackson is one of the few people in the country who could have pulled it off," adding that he was impressed that Jackson did what his government asked and never grandstanded.

While Perot's adventures in Vietnam and Iran are larger-than-life, they represent only a small chapter in the story of his involvement in governmental affairs. He has been an equally eager participant in domestic affairs, notably in the state of Texas. Future Lone Star history books are likely to reverberate with tales of Ross Perot's zealous war on drugs and passionate campaign against apathy in education.

Perot addressed the Texas state legislature in 1984. Topic: the need for educational reform.

Perot was still in Turkey during the final phases of the Iranian jail break when he was appointed by Governor Bill Clements to lead the Texas war on drugs. At the time, Perot knew so little about the topic one friend quipped he probably didn't know what drug paraphernalia was. But Perot learned quickly, devoting all his time to self-education and a total commitment to the cause.

As one reporter wrote in the April 16, 1980, Dallas *Times-Herald*, "Under most business leaders, a drug commission would have fluttered briefly in the post-election breezes of good intentions, then disappeared. But in the year since he was named to head the commission, Perot has emerged from a self-confessed ignorance about the netherworld of narcotics into an increasingly visible posture throughout the state."

"He was a perfect person to recruit. He's not a passive, superficial kind of guy. . . . Ross has that kind of drive and enthusiasm," Governor Clements told the Dallas *Morning News* on January 29, 1986.

Perot was on a mission, and he took the entire 14-member drug commission with him. Every four to six weeks, the crew would march to Perot's "drug central" at EDS headquarters for a full day of work. From his deep pockets, Perot shelled out nearly $2 million that covered, among other things, the expense of bringing experts from every angle of the field— police, attorneys, and physicians—to educate the committee. He hired consultants and visited state mental hospitals and prisons. In time, Ross Perot became an expert on the subject of drugs and drug use in Texas.

In the media and before politicians, schools, and church groups, Perot gave fiery, eye-opening speeches. The April 9, 1980, Dallas *Times-Herald* noted Perot's admonition to parents not to take the word of their children. "In 100 percent of the cases, they lie," he said. He advised parents to take teens suspected of drug use to an eye, ear, nose, and throat specialist to check for throat lesions.

A week later, the *Times-Herald* covered Perot's address to the Greater Dallas Crime Commission. Of the drug trade, Perot said, "It is a cancer on our nation. It is a $63 billion business that has no books, no taxes. Everything is under the table."

Perot described wealthy Texas families where children pawn jewels and silver to support drug habits; smuggling operations that paid Texas college girls $200 to hide drugs inside their bodies to smuggle them in from Mexico; drug transactions so large that $100 bills were weighed rather than counted.

"This is not Woodstock. This is Dallas, Texas," Perot told a church congregation. (Dallas *Times-Herald*, April 9, 1980.)

Drug abuse can be curtailed, Perot believes, but tough measures are required in order to do so.

Texas, Perot asserted, must ban "head shops" and must blacklist "soft" judges. For the education of his audience of Texas mayors, Perot demonstrated a "power hitter," a device designed to force smoke into the lungs of a marijuana user in order to increase the high. Perot showed the mayors phony soda and oil cans sold that are explicitly designed to conceal drugs, and that are available at paraphernalia stores.

As reported by the Dallas *Morning News* on April 15, 1980, Perot explained to the assembled mayors that "A world exists for our children that we have no knowledge of." He added, "Even New Jersey had made [certain drug paraphernalia] illegal."

Before the fight was over, Perot hammered a series of five "get tough" drug laws through the state legislature, threatening to brand those who opposed him as favoring drugs. Through the laws, prison sentences in the already strict state of Texas became even longer, both for drug dealers and users. Even the wiretap laws, opposed by liberals and hardly supported by law enforcement, were approved.

"When drug dealers look at those laws, they're going to get out of Texas," Perot proclaimed in the December 1988 issue of *Texas Monthly*.

The tough Texas laws and Perot's education-oriented bombardment of his drug message received national attention. Indeed, Perot was a key player in First Lady Nancy Reagan's nationwide assault on drugs. According to the *Texas Monthly* article, Perot, aware of Mrs. Reagan's concern over children using drugs, afforded her the opportunity to improve her image by getting involved in his crusade. Following a White House meeting, the very popular "Just Say No" campaign was formulated.

Top and above: First Lady Nancy Reagan, eager to establish her position on drug use, enlisted Perot's aid. These photos are from a 1983 antidrug dinner.

While it would appear Perot enjoyed great success in his battle against drugs, some observers questioned his tactics, and more. Few complained about the idealistic goals of the new laws, but many believed they were severely lacking in appropriations to carry them out and had little practical value.

Terral Smith, an Austin, Texas, Republican who chaired the subcommittee that worked on Perot's bills, told *Texas Monthly* in December 1988, "[Perot's initiatives] required a real financial commitment to law enforcement and to prisons. To really make a dent, it would take close to a billion dollars. That wasn't even discussed."

Perot's campaign also did little to endear him to the Texas underclass. Emotions became frayed and at one point, a Dallas *Times-Herald* columnist said Perot suggested cordoning off some of the worst sections of Dallas for a house-to-house search and destruction of drugs and weapons.

While Perot denies making those comments, another reporter, Peter Elkind, who wrote a number of in-depth articles on Perot, said in a *New York Times* article that he asked Perot if he'd made such a statement, and Perot didn't deny it. The *Times* article said Perot did not recall being asked by Elkind about searches.

"He explicitly defended the need for radical action," Elkind stated in the April 27, 1992, *New*

York Times. "This guy believes in the straight-line solutions to problems. Niceties like civil liberties and international law shouldn't get in the way."

Perot appeared to be overstepping his bounds, actually reaching into the realm of law enforcement. He gave the impression he was either privy to inside information or developing private information sources on his own. He talked about planned assassinations of undercover narcotics agents and himself, and at one point sought a heliport at his home to create a quick escape route.

He even hid two Tyler, Texas, undercover narcotics agents in his home to protect them from hired assassins. At that time, the agents were under investigation for alleged involvement in drug trafficking. Perot initially denied knowledge of the pair's whereabouts, but another agent was forced to reveal the information under oath in court.

Perot defended his actions, claiming the officers, one of whom had already been wounded by a shotgun blast, were in serious danger.

Years after his initiation into the war on drugs, Perot again found himself working with the Dallas Police Department. This time he was involved in the crossfire of a three-way battle among the police officers, city council, and local black leaders.

Equality and fair treatment for all were keynotes of
Perot's race-relations efforts in Dallas.

Racial tensions were heating up in Dallas
between 1986 and 1988. Things began to go bad
when a shootout took the lives of a white police
officer and a black criminal suspect.

"The whole scene changed at that time,"
said Monica Smith, police association president,
quoted in the Dallas *Morning News* on May 8,
1988. "Sure, prior to Officer [Gary] Blair's death,

we got spat on, we got challenged. But the very night that occurred, on every shift in every part of the city, officers were confronted with people saying, 'you can't arrest me, you kill people for no reason at all.' It seemed like a reflection of so much of what those so-called leaders of the minority community were saying."

Instances of assaults on officers increased, but so did cases of excessive police force, including the police shootings of two senior citizens, one of whom was a crime watch volunteer.

The Dallas city council sided with minority leaders and called for a redefinition of the deadly force policy. The council also approved a police reform plan that included a strengthened civilian review board.

The police department revolted after the shooting deaths of three Dallas officers in a six-week period. At the time black leaders were trying to once again strengthen the powers of the civilian review board.

When Perot was brought in, police morale was at a new low. Monica Smith was considering using collective bargaining to force an agreement with the city. However, Perot had another plan. Whatever that plan was going to be, it was formulated in a city where citizens were sharply divided in their opinions of Perot. The Dallas *Morning News* reported in its May 8, 1988, edition that some hailed Perot as "a non-partisan defender of truth, justice and the

American way" while others accused him of "acting as an unelected right-wing political czar trying to reshape Dallas and Texas in his own image."

Perot convinced Smith that the police department lacked public support of collective bargaining. He persuaded her to lobby for increases in staffing and suggested threatening the city council with a petition drive that would call for a referendum on abolishing the citizen review board. City leaders knew putting the question up for a vote would only serve to polarize an already racially tense Dallas.

The compromise approved by the council called for limiting the powers of the review board. That compromise was drafted by Perot's attorney.

With the city and officers in agreement, Perot was left with the task of pitching the idea to Dallas's black leaders. At a meeting with more than 100 black ministers, Perot called for a new relationship between the Dallas Police Department and the black community. That idea involved inviting officers into the churches to meet the residents of Dallas and creating a new mutual understanding of needs.

"We think it's important for police officers who work in this part of town to know the ministers, to know the congregation, to know the people they serve," Perot said in a June 1, 1988, story in the Dallas *Morning News*.

Perot's methods during his war on drugs and his manner of interceding in the Dallas police negotiations varied greatly, but shared the same ultimate outcome—success. In one he used fiery speeches and in the other tactical advice. In both, he knew which buttons to push.

When describing himself, Perot is known for using the analogy of an oyster. He has said on numerous occasions that he once considered himself the pearl in the oyster. But now he says he would rather be viewed as the grain of sand that irritated the oyster and caused it to produce the pearl.

Governor Mark White needed a grain of sand when appointing the Select Committee on Public Education. And just as Bill Clements had done during the war on drugs, White turned to Ross Perot.

Perot was given the task of turning the state's struggling public school system into a pearl. But to accomplish his task, he first had to irritate the giant oyster, which he saw as a "good ol' boy" network of football coaches and administrators mired in a school system of complacency and incompetence. His preferred tactic was clear in a quote that appeared in the October 3, 1983, Dallas *Times-Herald*: "I try to make strong, blunt statements so that people will react. That's the game that's being played."

As head of the school reform panel, Perot did not endear himself to many in the education business. He not only indicted the entire public school board for ineffectiveness, but he branded many in the teaching profession as the "least-literate work force in the industrialized world." (*Los Angeles Times,* December 22, 1991.) And what shocked some Texans most of all was Perot's willingness to take shots at one of the state's cherished institutions, high school football.

Ross Perot was on a mission. He committed himself to turning the tables on the Texas public schools. He began his campaign with a belief that education is the cornerstone of the future. In the business world, he often was quoted as saying America's success hinges on the creation of jobs, innovative and sound engineering practices, and education. A man on welfare costs the government money and cheats it out of tax dollars. Investing in quality education makes good economic sense.

"You can send [a man] to Harvard a whole lot cheaper than you can send him to Huntsville," Perot said. (Dallas *Morning News,* January 6, 1984.)

Perot outlined four basic principles the education committee would address through legislation: reserving the school day for learning; placing quality teachers in every classroom; enlisting parental support for education; and building strong primary schools. Perot viewed the early school years as particularly critical to a student's future success.

It was when Perot expanded on his four-point plan for reshaping Texas schools that he started making enemies fast.

Among the first were teachers, and for that matter the entire system of Texas teachers' colleges. Perot claimed that, of every five graduates of a Texas education school, only one is qualified to teach. Those other four incompetents make their way into Texas classrooms and "thousands of students are damaged every day" while administrators "hold hands" and ignore it.

"How does a school [of education] rationalize these illiterate, incompetent people for a teacher's certificate?" Perot asked the dean of Trinity University education college during a commission hearing. (Dallas *Times-Herald*, October 3, 1983.)

Frank talk characterized Perot's public stance regarding teacher competency in Texas.

As he did during his crusade against drugs, Perot used stirring speeches to galvanize support for education reform in Texas. But Perot also took to heart some of the lessons he learned in his antidrug crusade. Rather than using citizen groups to carry his fight to the legislature, he signed a powerful and high-priced professional lobbying team, at his own expense.

Thanks largely to Perot's efforts, a landmark education reform bill finally passed in the Texas legislature in July 1984. The version of the approved bill included only minimal amendments to Perot's proposal. He won almost every battle, at least up to that point.

The reform package included required competency testing of teachers; a merit pay system for teacher performance; mandated prekindergarten programs for disadvantaged four-year-olds; and the controversial "no pass, no play" rule for students involved in extracurricular activities, including athletics.

Not all of Perot's bill squeaked through the legislature unscathed. A provision to replace the elected State Board of Education with an appointed board was modified, as was a proposal for massive redistribution of state aid. Further, a Texas House-Senate compromise managed to take the teeth out of proposals to reduce class size and eliminate automatic annual pay raises for teachers.

Regardless of these compromises, Perot's efforts had paid off. The July 2, 1984, Dallas

Morning News quoted a pleased Linus Wright, Dallas school superintendent, as saying that the provisions are "the most comprehensive reforms in education in Texas since 1949."

Early in the fight, Perot was intent on abandoning a 27-member elected school board. He claimed it was too cumbersome to accomplish anything even remotely resembling the reforms he deemed necessary to bring Texas education back from the dead. He even swore he would not accept anything less on the issue and would exert all of his influence to kill any compromise that kept the current board in power.

"There is a reason behind that rigid, inflexible position," Perot told the Dallas *Times-Herald*, May 22, 1984. "You've got to have strong management to run an $8.3 billion business."

Under the approved law, the governor would appoint a 15-member State Board of Education to replace the current group of 27. However, after four years it would again become an elected position.

The redistribution plan was hailed by Perot's chief lobbyist, Rick Salwen, as the most substantial change in school financing in recent memory, even though the final product accomplished less than half of the committee's recommendations. Perot said throughout his campaign if the reform act did not include a means of sharing the wealth among rich and poor districts, it would be only a matter of time before a court ordered the move.

Perot's reforms, the most sweeping in Texas school history, had a tremendous impact on teachers and sports programs. Long after Perot's panel disbanded, cries were heard around the state from teachers, students, coaches, and parents. Bumper stickers that proclaimed "I Will Not Brake for Ross Perot" began showing up around the state, and Perot was denounced up and down Texas.

Abraham Lincoln (background) was largely self-educated; Perot wants things better for today's students.

Teachers felt the heat of the Perot education package as much as anyone. A survey commissioned by Perot's committee estimated the new teacher competency tests would usher five to ten percent of all Texas teachers out of classrooms. But according to the National Education Association, the country's largest teacher organization, Perot's plan would force out thousands of quality teachers. As the Dallas *Morning News* reported on February 5, 1985, what Perot called "absolutely essential," one leading educator called "asinine."

While the impact of the new tests could only be guessed at, some critics pointed to a 1983 pilot examination in Houston, where 3,200 teachers tested their skills on a teacher training institution admissions test. The test was geared toward college sophomores. However, the test group had a 62 percent failure rate in the reading portion while only 54 percent passed the math section. There were even widespread instances of cheating.

"It has put a cloud over the profession. It is going to leave the impression that if you can't pass the test, you can't teach—most teachers think that is wrong," said Mike Morrow, executive director of the Association of Texas Professional Teachers. (Dallas *Morning News*, February 5, 1985.)

But teacher testing did not create nearly as great a stir around Texas as the "no pass, no play" law. Tinkering with high school football in Texas is not recommended, but Perot did not intend the rule to hit only athletes.

"We have to recover the school day for learning," Perot told *D Magazine* in a January 1984 interview. "We sell [school-sponsored] cookies, we sell ribbons, we sell balloons—and if you're not selling *D Magazine* in our schools, I assure you're missing a good marketing opportunity. Everything takes priority over the classroom."

The real furor over "no pass, no play" erupted on the athletic fields across Texas. The law required teachers to keep track of the work of all students involved in extracurricular activities. After the end of each six-week period, any student not passing all courses with a 70 or better was denied participation in that activity during the next six-week grading period.

Opponents, many of them high school coaches, claimed the law discriminated against those involved in activities. Furthermore, it ignored those students who weren't involved with school functions or athletics, and more often than not they were worse students.

At the completion of the first grading period after the law took effect, newspapers were filled with accounts of football teams that lost half their offensive lines. Small schools were complaining they were hardest hit. The rule compounded an existing problem of a lack of students to field a team. There also were concerns about the impact of the rule on borderline students who were already struggling with college-prep classes.

The October 7, 1984, Dallas *Morning News* quoted a coach who lost four of his players after the first six-week grading period: "This is not a problem for an A and B student. But if there is a player that makes a 72 or 73 in algebra and he can take a higher math when he is looking at his next subjects, he may channel into something else that won't be such a risk. That is not the best thing, but that will be the reality in a lot of cases."

Perot had little sympathy: "Anytime someone has a problem, they can come up with an alibi or an excuse," he told the November 10, 1985, *Morning News*. "That's all it is. If a student doesn't have a learning disability, passing all his classes in school is not that difficult. There's a solution to all this: study. All we want is to keep a balance and set the proper priorities."

But the fight against the reforms remained intense. Within six months, the Texas legislature was back in session discussing new proposals to soften Perot's legislation. Teacher competency testing, school discipline, smaller class sizes, and merit pay scales all were on the agenda. So was the "no pass, no play" rule, which a Senate panel altered so that grades were reported weekly, and failing grades called for only a one-week suspension from a school activity.

"If we turn everything over to [the state legislature] now, we will be turning the clock back on education in Texas," Perot said in the January 7, 1985, Dallas *Morning News*.

Governor White, who had appointed Perot to head the commission, agreed with his man and stood by the reforms. However, as White's next election campaign loomed closer, the pressure levied against him mounted. Perot lost a major referendum fight to fill the State Board of Education with members to be appointed by the governor; worse, the first elected board leader was a Perot antagonist.

Reform opponents swore to fight White's bid for re-election. They did, and they were successful. Bill Clements moved back into the governor's mansion and over a period of years Perot's reforms were softened. However, he maintained his efforts throughout and certainly won the major battle of alerting Texas to the perils of what he viewed as a dilapidated education system.

"Some little self-interest thing you're doing, I wilt as quickly as anybody. But on the principle that three million kids should get a decent education in Texas, that's easy to fight for and to keep fighting for," Perot told the Dallas *Morning News*, January 29, 1986.

Perot's activism is hard to ignore. His friends and foes alike will agree that he has made a deep mark on Texas. To some observers, he functions like an undisciplined sort of Rambo figure. To others, he's a crusader who always takes that extra step to accomplish his goals.

Even Perot's enemies must admit that the man has augmented his political activism with a remarkable level of philanthropy. Over the years, the Perot Foundation has donated more than $120 million to charitable causes. And Perot has not given this money thoughtlessly, and certainly not so that he can write it off on his tax returns. In fact, for years he refused to take legitimate tax deductions for his charitable donations, saying he said he felt he owed it to his country.

Perot does not involve himself in a charitable effort until he is completely satisfied of its worthiness.

PEROT: MAN AS LEGEND

Perot is a career philanthropist who receives hundreds of requests for money each day. Whether he gives away one dollar or a million, it is for a patriotic reason, either stemming from his love of America or his love of Texas. Perot firmly believes he can use his money to make a difference in society and in people's lives.

"I ignore any kidding about my love of country," Perot told the *Saturday Evening Post* in April 1983. "My interest in this country is deep, complex and very well thought out. Simply put, we just can't take from our country, we must also give. It is easy to criticize the dirty river. It's a challenge to clean it up."

He added, "The love of our country is very fundamental to the success of our great country. That's what every last one of us must keep in mind."

A terrible 1988 forest fire at Yellowstone National Park, a topic of conversation during the course of Peter Elkind's December 1988 *Texas Monthly* interview with Perot, illustrates the billionaire's grasp of his responsibility to use his fortune for the common benefit of all. Early in the course of the fire, a friend warned Perot that the government's policy of allowing fires to burn in certain cases could endanger the entire park. Perot approached Washington and was assured that the policy was sound and that, in fact, occasional fires were *good* for the forest. The fire continued to burn and Perot could only watch, helpless, as half of the forest's natural beauty and resources were destroyed.

Instead of blaming the government policy that apparently allowed the ruination of so much priceless land, Perot blamed himself. "I'm better than that," he said later. "I could have gotten that fire put out."

Perot believed he had the power to force action early on where inaction was the norm: "I could've raised enough hell that they would've *had* to put the fire out. I know how media sensitive they are [in Washington]."

Some argue that Perot's greatest business failures were originally engineered as charity, designed with the ultimate goal of saving the entire nation from possible catastrophe. A case in point involves du Pont, Glore Forgan & Co., an enormous brokerage firm that was a cornerstone of the New York Stock Exchange. Perot was approached to help save the faltering company in 1970; to that point in his career, he had never experienced business failure. He was told that for a mere $5 million he could rescue the company, and that without his help the entire stock exchange could fall. Even President Nixon, who maintained close ties to Perot, had his aides encourage the purchase. At one point, someone actually attempted to coax Perot into buying the entire stock exchange.

Convinced his help was desperately needed, Perot accepted the challenge. However, the $5 million price tag soon turned into $10 million, and before the affair was over, Perot was $60 million in the hole and ready to give up and get out.

The goal that motivated Perot in the du Pont affair—to save jobs and stimulate the economy—also motivated him in 1984, when he merged his company, EDS, with General Motors (an arrangement described in the second chapter of this book). He looked at GM and saw a once-prosperous company in danger of falling to pieces. He felt that EDS could prevent the collapse and massive job loss that would result.

"At first we weren't interested [in the merger]," Perot told the Dallas *Morning News*, January 29, 1986. "I told Roger Smith I was working on education reform and that was a lot more important to me than selling EDS. I told them they'd have to wait."

GM continued to persist and Perot was swayed: "Finally we decided there was nothing we could do that would be more interesting than trying to help General Motors realize its full potential."

Unfortunately, after the merger Perot found himself unable to take the control he desired and needed to meet his ultimate goal. A power struggle eventually led to his losing control of EDS.

It is true that Perot stood to gain tremendously had the du Pont and GM deals evolved according to plan. However, it also is true that both ventures, if successful, could have brought about great benefits for the nation. These philanthropic ventures, though unconventional, were also apparently sincere, and a far cry from presenting a check at a black-tie affair simply to get one's photo in the paper.

Another area that interests Perot is historic documents; he explored it because he felt it was incumbent on him to preserve history for children, to ensure that they receive a fair opportunity to appreciate the heritage of this country.

The November 12, 1984, issue of *People Weekly* included a story on Perot's $1.5 million dollar purchase and exhibit of an original 1297 copy of the Magna Carta, the 1215 charter granted by King John of England that guaranteed certain civil and political liberties to English barons. *People* quoted Perot as remarking, "We are very fortunate to have our freedoms in this country and it is very important for the children to know this. The day I see the exhibit and see a large crowd of children captivated and learning, that day I will be happy. That's the why of it."

Perot's copy of the Magna Carta is only one of 17 known to exist, and is one of only two not retained in England (the other is owned by Australia). Clearly, the document is a very valuable item, but to Perot its value extends far beyond the sale price, its age, or numbers of copies in circulation.

As Perot explained to the Dallas *Morning News*, September 26, 1984, "I was interested in it because it was the document that first gave people individual freedom. It was the basis for our Constitution and our system of government."

Perot sent the document to the University of Texas for physical rehabilitation and arranged for a customized case, complete with proper lighting and temperature and humidity controls designed to aid in preservation. The document was exhibited at the Texas state fair and subsequently was put on national tour, with an emphasis on stops at schools. The eventual permanent home of the historic document will be in the rotunda of the National Archives.

Perot's fascination with historic documents did not end with the Magna Carta. An attempt to purchase the Emancipation Proclamation came to naught when he was outbid by publisher Malcolm Forbes (the going price was $297,000), but Texas historians were pleasantly surprised when Perot secured the purchase of the original deed to the township of Dallas. Many thought the paper had been lost. After the purchase, the Dallas *Morning News* quipped that with the document Perot could make official his claim for ownership of Dallas.

Besides historic documents, Perot is keenly interested in the arts and in research projects. He has contributed millions of dollars, for

Perot is driven by the concept of personal freedom—one explanation for his fervent interest in POWs.

instance, to research projects designed to develop new inventions.

But while recipients are grateful, they also feel the pressure. "World class" is a phrase common to Perot when discussing donations to any cause. If the potential recipient does not live up to Perot's standards of excellence, Perot has no qualms about rescinding his offer.

Journalist Peter Elkind wrote in the December 1988 issue of *Texas Monthly*, "[Perot] regards his charity as another form of investment, a sort of venture capital that he expects to yield improvement in the lot of mankind. Before turning over a penny, he details his expectations. To assure they will be met, he doles out gifts in installments."

Elkind illustrates his point through a story about Bishop College, a debt-ridden black school in Dallas whose supporters were desperate for Perot to help them keep the doors open. According to Elkind, however, Perot remained unconvinced that the college leadership could meet his lofty goals for greatness. So it was that Perot, the man who revitalized public education in Texas, the man whose first charitable donation in the early years of his wealth was $2.4 million to a predominantly black inner-city school district that needed special learning programs, let Bishop College die.

"The last thing those students need is anything second rate," Perot said.

Officials at the Dallas Arboretum and Botanical Society also are well aware of Perot's expectations. In 1985, Dallas city officials proposed a 15-year program to provide $30 million of $55 million needed to build what supporters claimed would be among the finest arboretums and botanical gardens in the nation. Grandiose plans included a visitors center, education and research facilities, an amphitheater for cultural events, restaurants, and several theme gardens with walking trails. The beauty of the facility would complement Dallas's plans to spend another $28 million on land in the downtown area to expand the city's planned Arts District.

"The facility we're proposing would provide the missing piece for Dallas—a place of natural beauty that everyone is proud of and can go to to enjoy nature," said Robert Tener, arboretum society president. (Dallas *Morning News*, October 27, 1985.)

Perot took an interest in the arboretum project, which needed an estimated $20 to $25 million from private sources. The arboretum chairman was his friend and neighbor, Ralph Rogers (later replaced by Tener). Perot had received $8 million settlement money over a land dispute, and offered the sum to the arboretum committee. As had been the case with many of Perot's other major philanthropic ventures, the arboretum had to meet certain conditions. Among the requirements placed on the arboretum when Perot gave his initial payment of $2 million was a demand for the successful collection of all monies needed to make the arboretum truly a "world class" garden.

In time, plans for the new botanical garden appeared to be complete. However, a local homeowners association was balking, claiming

the facility would be insensitive to both the
environment and to low-income residents who
could not afford the price of admission. The
association was also concerned with the
inevitable increase of traffic near the
arboretum.

As time passed, the arboretum committee
faced more than just angry homeowners. Hard
economic times forced Dallas officials to take a
closer look at priorities. Money was needed
badly to fund the police department and local
housing; the arboretum was quickly dropping
down the list. By the time Dallas officials cut
back on the project's funding, Ralph Rogers was
out as president of the arboretum society and
Robert Tener was in control.

It was clear to Perot that the world-class
arboretum he expected and demanded would
never materialize. With that in mind, he
rescinded his grant and demanded the return of
the $2 million. If he did not get the money, he
threatened a lawsuit.

Perot eventually settled with society officials.
He canceled the $6 million outstanding
donation money, but agreed to let the society
keep the $2 million.

"Two million is more than we had," one
council member told the August 8, 1988, edition
of the Dallas *Morning News*. "I'm just glad it
ended the way it did."

Perot became involved in another would-be
cultural event in 1982, when Dallas voters

If a philanthropic effort does not seem to be panning out as Perot would like, he'll withdraw support.

agreed to sell $28.6 million in bonds to build a new concert hall for the Dallas Symphony Orchestra. Projected total cost was $49.5 million. Perot had a close connection to the proposed hall—EDS president Morton Meyerson was chairman of the concert hall committee.

Perot considered Meyerson a dedicated and valued employee who worked an average of 60 hours a week and "contributed more to growth and profitability [of EDS] than any other individual in the company." (Dallas *Morning News*, November 1, 1984.)

To thank Meyerson for his service, Perot offered $10 million toward construction of the symphony hall. But there was a catch: In order to use Perot's money, the hall had to be named after Meyerson. Before the news conference announcing the donation, city and park district commissioners voted to name the facility The Morton H. Meyerson Symphony Center.

In a prepared statement Perot said, "Mort has played a leading role in the growth and success of EDS. Mort's name on the symphony hall will symbolize the thousands of men and women who worked with him to build EDS. Without them, this gift would not be possible."

Perot's gift was one of the largest ever made to any arts organization in America. Unfortunately, not long after construction began the project soared some $25 million over budget. It would now cost $75 million, not $49.5 million. However, the additional expenses were expected to cover enhancements such as a larger-size building, limestone exterior walls, marble lobby floors, and a special wood paneling for better appearance and acoustics. Perot did not balk.

"I told them I didn't want to get involved with it unless it was really a world-class operation, and they assured me it would be," Perot said. (Dallas *Morning News*, January 18, 1985.)

Another tale of Perot philanthropy tells of his about-face on funding research at a Texas medical school.

"I've never read about it in *Time* magazine or *The New York Times*. I have no knowledge that it's a great medical school," Perot told friend Ralph Rogers after being asked in 1985 to help fund research at the University of Texas Southwestern medical school in Dallas.

"I'm only interested in institutions that are or could become outstanding institutions in the nation." (*Texas Monthly*, December 1988.)

Later that year, in October 1985, Dr. Joseph Goldstein and Dr. Michael Brown, both connected to the Southwestern Medical Center, became Nobel Prize winners for medicine. The doctors developed and eventually gained approval for the drug Lovastatin, which evolved from their work on cholesterol metabolism. The drug, and the work of the two Texas doctors, was heralded as having the capability to save thousands of lives annually through a new treatment of strokes, heart attacks, and other diseases related to cholesterol.

The university health care center also was gaining national attention for other exploits,

Perot is very serious about his endeavors, but he is far from a stuffed shirt, as demonstrated by his delighted reaction to a gag during a 1987 Ross Perot roast.

including research on Alzheimer's disease, organ transplants, and genetic disorders. Perot was immediately impressed with Texas's first home-grown Nobel Prize winners and with the school that was one of only 11 in the nation to rank near the top in seven possible categories.

But Perot was not impressed with the level of attention these doctors were receiving in their home town. He and his wife, Margot, organized and hosted a gala reception.

The January 9, 1986, Dallas *Morning News* quoted a volunteer planner as saying, "There are really two purposes of the dinner. One is to honor Brown and Goldstein. The other is to make the business community more aware of the tremendous resource we have in the UT Health Science Center. [The Perots] wanted to make this best-kept secret better known to the business community in the city."

Shortly after the event the university announced that six months of negotiations were nearing completion and that news of a generous donation from Ross Perot would be forthcoming.

Perot said, "Right now I'm on the one-yard line of a donation even larger [than the $15 million donation to a San Antonio biotechnology park] to the Health Science Center in Dallas, to accelerate the work of its two Nobel Prize winners. I am serious about Texas having a worldwide impact on the health of people." (Dallas *Morning News*, January 13, 1988).

Perot pledged $20 million over a ten-year period, including $650,000 annually to support the research of Brown and Goldstein. However, it was more than just a gift. The arrangement called for half of all profits from licensing of all technologies devised through research supported by Perot to benefit the Perot Foundation.

Charles Sprague, president emeritus of the center, told the January 13, 1988, edition of the Dallas *Morning News*, "I hope people will hear that Mr. Perot insists on quality, and if he is willing to support the school, they would want to as well."

The Texas Research and Technology Foundation, a biotechnological research park created jointly by San Antonio and University of Texas System, is another beneficiary of Ross Perot's generosity. Perot was particularly impressed because the research park had the potential to create 2,000 new jobs in the south Texas area.

"All I ask you to do is make it the best in the world," Perot said. "There is no advantage to our people in building mediocre institutions in Texas." (Dallas *Morning News*, March 21, 1987.)

Many of Perot's philanthropic endeavors centered on education and the arts, and on the betterment of institutions in his beloved home state of Texas. But, like the botanical garden, not all were successful.

The Museum of the American Indian in New York City is one that got away. Perot never heard of the museum until he was asked to rescue it. A quick study of the museum and its collection convinced him that the institution deserved to be saved. More than that, he wanted to bring it to Dallas.

The February 23, 1985, edition of the Dallas *Morning News* quoted Perot as saying, "My perception of the collection—the way it's been described to me by scholars around the country—is that it's a one million-piece collection of how man changed from the top of the Aleutian Islands to the tip of South America. . . . It's the whole hemisphere. It's the finest museum in the world, as far as I'm concerned. It will be the only world-class museum we can possibly get in Texas."

Perot offered the museum $70 million for a new building in Dallas. Although no plans were set, he envisioned a sprawling ten-acre complex with room for outdoor pageants. Perot was willing to build the facility himself, but said he had plenty of support from fellow Texans eager to transplant the collection.

After talks began, a sudden snowball effect emerged and it appeared Dallas would become home to a truly astounding collection of Indian artifacts: Officials at the Peabody Museum of Archaeology and Ethnology at Harvard University announced they would approach Perot with an offer to move to Dallas.

The Peabody Museum Indian collection was revered by experts as one of the five finest in the country. Although not in financial trouble, it lacked proper display space.

When Perot heard about the possibility he was awestruck: "If you get the Indian museum in New York and the Peabody Museum together, that's it," he told the Dallas *Morning News*, June 29, 1985. "That's the most fantastic collection you can put together."

But throughout all the excitement, Perot refused to get too optimistic, and even called the deal with the Museum of the American Indian a "long shot." When giving the museum to New York City in 1916, its founder stipulated that it must remain in the city. And Perot knew that officials in New York City and in the state of New York, as well as the local business community, were willing to put up a fight to keep the museum where it was.

"I said [to the museum's trustees] 'if this thing can be done gracefully, I'm interested. If this thing turns into a mess, I don't want any part of it,'" Perot said. (Dallas *Morning News*, February 23, 1985.)

Perot agreed with museum trustees that this was not an outright purchase. It would remain a public institution with no private ownership of artifacts. And while he rejected a proposal to leave part of the collection in New York on a permanent basis, he did agree to continuously send works to the city for display.

His pledges pleased the trustees. In June 1985 they tentatively agreed to accept Perot's

The media spotlight is not new to Perot. He has received attention from business deals to charitable endeavors.

offer to move to Dallas. But, the plans remained tentative and the battle over the museum's location heated up. New York governor Mario Cuomo, philanthropist David Rockefeller, Vice President George Bush, and President Ronald Reagan came out in favor of keeping the museum in New York City.

The museum asked the state Supreme Court for permission to leave New York. But before a decision was handed down, Reagan ordered Chief of Staff Donald Regan to make arrangements to use the U.S. Customs House in Manhattan to house the old Indian collection. Perot objected to this plan, noting that it would cost taxpayers $30 million.

During two years of conflict, the museum laid off workers to prove financial hardship. It rejected Perot's offer and said it would explore other options, then turned around and asked Perot to renew his interest. Finally, in 1987, Perot had had enough. He retracted his offer on the grounds the museum had a viable alternative. Dallas did not become home to the ultimate museum of Indian culture.

Perot was not always at odds with New York City when it came to his charitable work. In fact, New Yorkers were more than a little surprised when they learned it was Ross Perot who anonymously donated 20 Tennessee walking horses to the city's police department. This $50,000 gift came complete with saddles, solid brass rosettes, and medallions. Perot even flew top police officials to a ranch in Corpus Christi, Texas, where they could inspect the new four-legged recruits. What could possibly have inspired a rich Texan to take a benevolent interest in the affairs of the New York City mounted police?

Perot was moved to make the gift after one of his teenage daughters admired the mounted police officers during a visit to the city. When she told her father that the city refused to fund replacement of aging horses, Perot went into action. A New York police officer quoted in the August 28, 1977, Dallas *Times-Herald* said, "Ross Perot convinced New Yorkers that not everyone in the world hated them."

Perot's charitable gestures continued. In 1985 he gave $100,000 to help promote a statewide Texas referendum to spend $1.43 billion on future water projects. Supporters of the bond issue said the future of Texas cities, farms, and industry was at stake.

Later that same year he vehemently refused to give a dime to the Dallas County Historical Commission to reopen the School Book Depository for public tours. Lee Harvey Oswald had crouched behind a Depository window when he shot and killed President John F. Kennedy in 1963. Perot refused to involve himself in the creation of what he regarded as a shrine for Oswald.

Funding libraries was something Perot did with regularity. In a week's time in 1986, for example, he made friends at both the University of Texas at Austin and the Dallas Public Library via generous donations.

For the university, Perot purchased what was heralded by the January 22, 1986, Dallas *Morning News* as the "last major privately held collection of English literary works, including the first book printed in English and rare masterworks of the greatest British authors from 1475 to 1700."

Three days later, the same newspaper reported on a gathering of 55 members of the Dallas Shakespeare Club, on hand at the Dallas Public Library for the unveiling of the rare first folio edition of Shakespeare's plays. Carrying an estimated price tag of $250,000, it is one of just two in the state of Texas.

Several Texas groups serving the poor also are thankful to Perot. In 1986 alone, he donated $38,500 to match money given by General Motors employees to the U.S. Marine Corps' Toys for Tots program, spent $1.5 million to buy a warehouse and offer it rent-free to the North Texas Food Bank, and promised the Salvation Army $100,000 a year indefinitely to help house and feed the poor at its new $16 million social service center. The food bank was expected to allow the organization to serve 150,000 more families every year through distribution of an additional five million pounds of food.

"The Perot Foundation stepped forward and said 'Why don't we just purchase the building and give it back to you rent-free,'" said Jack Gorman, food bank president. (Dallas *Morning News*, May 27, 1987.) "We were flabbergasted. It was an incredible, incredible gesture on their part to do this for us."

Perot also is known for using his funds to help individuals as well as groups of people. Early in his career he was known for helping family members of employees when they needed medical care. He made a similar gesture in 1987 when a 17-year-old boy disappeared in the Guadalupe River after a church bus was swept away by rising water.

The mother of John Bankston, Jr., said Perot stayed in contact with her while authorities searched for the body of her son, who was washed away while helping others get to safety. When Perot heard the search was abandoned, he offered his help. Helicopters, boats, dogs, and a dozen specially selected people were employed to help the Bankston family bring to an end the pain of not knowing exactly what happened to their son. However, after an unsuccessful two-week search that covered 30 miles of riverbank, the effort was halted.

Perot's philanthropic ventures have not gone unnoticed. He has received many accolades, including humanitarian awards and honorary degrees bestowed by universities. He was the first recipient of the Raoul Wallenberg Award for humanitarianism. Wallenberg was a Swedish diplomat who saved more than 100,000 Hungarian Jews from Nazi death camps during World War II before reportedly dying in a prison in the Soviet Union. Perot was chosen for the honor because of a lifetime of humanitarian efforts and his work on behalf of POWs.

Other honors include the Jefferson Award for public service for his work in education and the Iranian rescue, the 1985 Outstanding Philanthropist award from the Dallas chapter of the National Society of Fundraising Executives, and the 1985 National Philanthropist award from the parent chapter of the same organization.

However, Perot's most cherished award came when he was recognized by the Winston

Churchill Foundation of the United States for his lifelong accomplishments in business and public affairs. Perot was only the third recipient, following American statesman W. Averell Harriman in 1981 and British Prime Minister Margaret Thatcher in 1983. He was also the first businessman ever honored with the award named after British prime minister Winston Churchill, his all-time hero.

"Mr. Perot, like Churchill, is one of the remarkable men of his time," said John L. Loeb, Jr., president of the Churchill Foundation. "In public and private life, he has demonstrated the imagination, boldness and vigor which characterized Churchill." (Dallas *Morning News*, September 6, 1985.)

Perot's response to the award, as reported in the September 6, 1985, Dallas *Morning News*, was typically modest: "I don't feel I am in the same league as Mr. Harriman or Ms. Thatcher, but I am honored. I have always felt strongly about standing up for what I believe, and maybe that's what it is all about."

Even after the ultimate honor of receiving the Churchill award, Perot still maintains that he is an average man, not a legend.

"My life is like everybody else's," he said. "There's a thousand little things you do every day in a small way. I'm average. I'm not being modest there. There's nothing very special about me.

"Ninety-eight percent of my life is just like it was when I was broke. The other two percent is what you hear and read about." (Dallas *Morning News*, February 16, 1986.)

Perot's statement may be accurate; nevertheless, there is little doubt that that two percent of activity is exceptional. If there is a secret to his success, it may lie in his favorite Churchill quotation, one that Perot commonly uses to conclude his speeches: "Never give in. Never give in. Never. Never. Never."

Prince Charles awarded Perot the Winston Churchill Foundation medallion in 1985. The award had been given only twice previously.

CHAPTER 4

THE RUN FOR THE PRESIDENCY

"My feeling is if the
framers of the
Constitution are looking
down on all this
grass-roots [Perot
campaign] activity,
they must be smiling."
—Ross Perot
The New York Times National;
May 6, 1992

Opposite: Ross Perot—here addressing a rally—has always
described himself as a businessman, not a politician.

Over the past several years, people have encouraged Ross Perot to become involved in politics. He always responded that he was a businessman and that he felt he did more for the nation in that role.

"I decided years ago that my real role in life may be to create taxpayers," he told the Dallas *Morning News* in 1988.

But 1992 brought a change. Outspoken as always, Perot began to make speeches about what was wrong with the country, pointing to failures in government and its programs.

Cable News Network's Larry King asked Perot to appear for an hour on the February 20, 1992, edition of his show, *Larry King Live*. King began the interview by asking Perot why he did not run for President. Perot evaded the question. The discussion covered a spectrum of topics during the next hour; finally, at the end of the show, King gave it one more shot. "Under what circumstances would you run for the presidency?" King asked.

And Perot finally gave him an answer. "If voters in all 50 states put me on the ballot—not 48 or 49 states, but all 50—I will agree to run." But, he added, he doubted that would happen because the process is too complicated.

Two months later, draft Perot movements had sprung up in all 50 states. Perot himself set up a toll-free number for people to organize petition drives. Within the first month, that phone number had received about one and a

It was on Larry King's show that Perot revealed his conditions for running for President: He must be on the ballot in all 50 states.

half million calls. By mid-May, Perot had spent nearly a half million dollars of his own money financing the effort he repeatedly and publicly has said he believed would never get off the ground.

Although he has stated he would not run unless he is on the ballot in all 50 states, Perot has made all the noises of a full-blown candidate. In late March, Perot named former Vietnam POW James Stockdale as his "interim" running mate since a running mate is a ballot requirement in more than half the states. And he has resigned from two clubs with question-able membership practices.

In a March 18 appearance before the National Press Club, Perot detailed, in his down-home phrases, several of the nation's ills. He has brought forth many of the same themes in speeches and interviews since.

"We're four trillion dollars in debt," he told the National Press Club. "We owe another five trillion we don't like to talk about. Just kind of keep it down there in the basement. . . . The additional debt piled up in 1992, just this one year, the election year, will exceed the total expenditures for the federal government for the first 155 years of our country's existence.

"The total national debt was only one trillion dollars in 1980, when President Reagan took office. It is now four trillion dollars. Maybe it was voodoo economics. Whatever it was, we are now in deep voodoo, I'll tell you that.

"We spend over four hundred billion dollars a year on education, including colleges, yet we rank at the bottom of the industrialized world in terms of academic achievement. We have the largest number of functional illiterates in the industrialized world. . . . We spend a lot on education—it doesn't work.

"We spend more than anybody else on health care, and yet we rank behind 15 nations in life expectancy and 22 other nations on infant mortality. We've got five percent of the world's population, 50 percent of the world's cocaine users. Until we get rid of that, we're going nowhere.

Perot spoke at the National Press Club, outlining some of the problems the nation faces today, including poor education and health care and a paralyzed government.

"We've got the murder capital of the United States here [in Washington, D.C.]. Fifth and sixth graders in this city: 31 percent of them have witnessed a shooting, 43 percent have witnessed a mugging, 67 percent have witnessed a drug deal, and 75 [percent] have witnessed an arrest.

"Today we have a government in gridlock. . . . Daily, we watch with fascination as Congress and the White House finger point, shout, fight with one another like children. Recently it's been more like mud wrestling, as far as I'm concerned."

Perot doesn't deal in specifics when he talks about solutions to these problems. In a March 29, 1992, interview with the Dallas *Morning News,* Perot said he would not talk specifically about solutions until he had the time to research them and think them out clearly. "I will not sound-bite complex issues."

He stated during NBC's *Meet the Press* on May 3, 1992, "Right now I'm detailing all these positions. This whole effort is less than two months old, virtually all of my time has been spent with volunteers working on a 50-state petition signing effort. . . . What I'm trying to do now is get all these specifics put together."

But at the speech before the National Press Club, Perot did offer what he called "a few basics" for change.

"We need a growing job base to produce a growing tax base. We need growing companies to keep America at work. We can help in the government level by ceasing the adversarial practices for business and not getting our pockets picked at international trade negotiations. In our international competitors who are winning, there is an intelligent, supportive relationship between government and business. We'd better study it. We'd better copy it. We'd better improve on it.

"Our education system has to be the finest in the world. Let's stop reading to the children in school [to create political photo opportunities]. Let's stop having two-day summits with governors that don't amount to anything. Every day is precious and we just talk about it.

"Our current tax system is like an old inner tube with a thousand patches. I suggest we throw it out and start with a blank sheet of paper.

"We're divided by racial strife. Look, we're not Japan, where everybody's the same race, the same religion, same background, same philosophy. We're a melting pot, right? OK, we ought to love one another. That takes care of most of us. Then for the guys who can't quite cross that bridge, we ought to get along with one another, because divided teams lose and united teams win."

Many of these ideas are not new to anyone who has listened to Perot over the years. In 1988, Perot said the way to cut the defense budget was to make Europe and Japan pay for their military defense. He said each nation would provide savings of about $100 billion.

Recently, Perot has put forth other ideas, including rescinding Congress's authority to raise taxes. If a tax hike is needed, Perot said, it should go before the public for a vote.

A presidential candidate draws enormous media attention. Perot answered questions in Washington, D.C., and met with the American Society of Newspaper Editors.

He has also proposed an electronic town hall so voters could give their feedback to government on a variety of subjects. In areas where the technology is not yet available for viewer feedback, the telephone could be used. Perot said the town hall would prevent elected officials from losing touch with the people, whom he calls the owners of the company.

Perot has admitted that serving in government in an elected office would be somewhat alien to him. "I am tiptoeing into a world now where nobody gets things done,"

Perot said in a March 26, 1992, interview with the Dallas *Morning News.* "I live in a world of action, not talk." But Perot has stated he will take the job, or at least undertake the task of running for it, if the average American (through the petition drives) asks him to give it a shot. Perot noted, however, that the presidency is not something he has ever aspired to.

He told CBS's *60 Minutes* on March 29, 1992, "I wouldn't give you three cents to go up there. It's phony, it's artificial. They put you in a bubble, and here's what happens to [you]—it won't happen if I get stuck up there, I promise you that—they put you up there inside a bubble and all these people start feeding you stuff inside the bubble and pretty soon you don't know what is happening in real life."

Perot believes he is tough enough to withstand the rigors of the campaign, including the attacks and charges that might be leveled at him.

"Look, this kind of little Chinese fire drill stuff is nothing compared to the risks I've taken in my life," Perot was quoted in the May 3, 1992, Washington *Post.* "When you've got your life on the line, when you're walking down the streets of Tehran and everybody is saying . . . on loudspeakers. 'We're going to cut off the hands of the Americans. . . .' Your fingers tingle. I don't want to bore you with this stuff, but just having someone misrepresent who you are is like one mosquito at a picnic of 10,000 people.

This is nothing. This is schoolgirl stuff that all these guys are whining about."

Many, including Bush's campaign staff, said Perot has not yet seen the type and quantity of questions the press can throw at candidates for high office. But Perot said the campaign maneuvers and snipes, at least by the Republicans, started early. For several years, Perot and his son have been involved in a project to expand the Alliance Airport in Fort Worth, Texas. The two own much of the property around the airport. After Perot's announcement on the Larry King show, Perot said, the federal funding for the project was suddenly put on hold.

Federal officials have stated for the record that there was no political pressure to drag out the project. Perot thought otherwise, and although the delay didn't hurt him, he said it did hurt the people of the region who needed jobs.

Perot has said he will not engage in the negative campaigning that has been such a part of recent campaigns. He told *The New York Times* (May 6, 1992), "I hate the mud wrestling in politics. I think it's obscene. The one thing we have now is a system that will almost completely weed out anybody that you'd want as a presidential candidate."

If he does run, Perot also told *The New York Times* (March 7, 1992), "What you see is what you get. . . . I'm not going to be one of those people who hires handlers and image makers." He stressed he will not change his positions to please anyone.

That could cost him some votes from environmentalists. He believes the economy must be improved, even if the environment suffers. Perot has said it is everyone's job to protect the planet. But an article in the May 3, 1992, Washington *Post* quotes Perot, "I'm pragmatic. If there's a choice between survival and protecting the planet, we will pillage and plunder the planet, if it gets that basic.

"Let's assume you don't have a job and I don't have a job, and the only thing we can do is cut every tree in our area and ship it to Japan to feed our children. We're going to want to cut every tree in the area to ship it to Japan to feed our children. . . . Nobody will think about the spotted owl if they're starving, except maybe to eat him."

At first, political pundits discounted the hoopla immediately following Perot's Larry King appearance, but by the end of April, polls began to show that if the election were held then, it would be a close three-way race. Some polls reported Perot had surpassed Democrat Bill Clinton; others showed him in a virtual dead heat with President George Bush.

Voters nationwide quoted in newspapers and on television seemed to validate the polls.

Perot has stirred up grass-roots support. Here, volunteers call voters from his campaign headquarters in Dallas.

For many voters, it did not matter that they did not agree with some of Perot's positions on certain issues (for example, abortion or gun control). For others, the anti-incumbent sentiment was strong enough to push them into the Perot camp.

Perot's army of volunteers comes from sources that apparently had never been actively involved in politics before. And their reasons are as varied as their backgrounds.

Merrick Okamoto, a 31-year-old stockbroker who works in the Irvine, California, office to draft Perot, told *Time* magazine on April 20, 1992, "People who deny Perot's popularity just don't get it. This movement is about choice. People can't stand another four years of gridlock."

The April 30, 1992, *Wall Street Journal* quoted Ronnie Ellen, a 64-year-old Broadway show girl turned diamond cutter: "I like his ideas," she said, "perhaps because I think a lot like him."

A farmer in London, Kentucky, who has always been a Republican, gave his reason for supporting Perot to *The New York Times* on April 29, 1992: "I couldn't name a single issue of his, but I'm probably going to vote for him because we've got a bunch of sayers and no doers in Washington right now."

But is Perot truly a political outsider? Many who watch government and politics question whether Perot can lay claim to that label. Although he has not served in government, Perot is said to have had close ties to President Richard Nixon, to Oklahoma Senator David Boren, and to at least two Texas governors— Republican Bill Clements and Democrat Mark White.

In the case of Nixon, the Chicago *Tribune* reported on May 8, 1992, that Perot was the "ultimate insider." The article states that Nixon-era documents in the National Archives, reviewed by the Associated Press, show the connection.

"The documents say that between 1969 and 1973 Perot requested and received at least three private meetings with Nixon, attended eight White House social events and sometimes had contact with the White House as frequently as once a week."

The *Tribune* article also quotes a 1988 oral history interview with former Nixon special counsel Charles Colson. "I don't know anybody in the whole four years I was in the White House who was able to muscle himself in quicker into the president's own confidence."

The relationship between Perot and Senator Boren is long-standing, according to an October 18, 1990, *Wall Street Journal* article. "Their friendship goes back many years. Their daughters attended the Hockaday School in Dallas together. They each say they . . . consult periodically on issues ranging from tax policy to foreign affairs."

As to the Texas governors, Perot was involved in two crusades in Texas.

From 1979 to 1981, he worked with Governor Clements in a war on drugs. Clements appointed Perot to head a committee to look at stopping the flow of drugs across the Texas–Mexico border. Instead, Perot turned it into a crusade, tackling the drug problem across the state. He sent the Texas legislature a series of bills that, among other things, toughened the state's drug laws, already considered stiff by national standards. But the experts said the crusade failed, mainly because the committee did not include in the new laws a mechanism for funding the programs. As a result, drug dealers were not hindered because they had little fear of being caught.

Perot also reportedly had a hand in the "Just Say No" program of Nancy Reagan in the early 1980s.

In 1983 and 1984 Perot was tapped by Governor White to head a committee to look at education in Texas. Perot took the task to heart. Although not an outstanding student himself, the importance of a good education had been instilled in Perot from the time he was very young. That committee looked at problems in the state education system and came up with one proposal that had many in Texas fighting mad. "No pass, no play" was a plan barring a student-athlete from participating in athletics if he or she failed an academic course. A similar plan was put into effect for other extra-curricular activities.

Perot does not consider these instances the acts of a political insider, but rather the actions of a good citizen devoting time to his country. This attitude illustrates the philosophy that motivates Perot's run for the presidency: A man who has benefited from a nation should give back to that nation.

Ross Perot Speaks

Running for President is a complicated and laborious task. Perhaps the most difficult part of the process is fielding questions on the various important issues that face America today, from taxes and abortion to jobs and foreign affairs. Over the years, Ross Perot—in interviews and speeches—has spoken on many of these issues. Following is a compendium of some of his views on a wide range of topics.

On Abortion

"When that comes up, you will never just hear me say woman's choice. You will always hear me say, never forget, we aren't rabbits, we are thinking, reasoning human beings, and every human life is precious. . . . Now it is absolutely irresponsible for two thinking, reasoning human beings to get drunk, get high, get pregnant and get an abortion just because they act like rabbits."
—Washington *Post*, May 3, 1992

"[It would] be far better to get that procedure done properly than to pay the huge costs that could occur from the infections and the problems that could occur from doing it some other way."
—On whether taxpayers should pay for abortions for poor women who can't get them any other way; *Meet the Press*, May 3, 1992

On Affirmative Action

"It's got its pluses and minuses. It produces stress in society. The plus is it cleans up the inequity. That's—that's good. The minus is all the people who were more qualified and got passed over who probably didn't have any negative feelings based on race start developing them. There's only one long-term solution, and that is education, education, education."
—*Meet the Press,* May 3, 1992

On George Bush

"We spent ten years creating Saddam Hussein; we gave him billions [of dollars]. Our current President's fingerprints are all over giving him the billions, all the way up to the spring of [1990]—before . . . August when we put the troops in the desert."
—*60 Minutes,* March 29, 1992

"If [Bush] spends time working with [the Department of Education] instead of reading to children to get TV coverage, we'll be headed somewhere."
—Los Angeles *Times,* December 22, 1991

"I said we all have different styles. So I'm not criticizing his style at all."
—On President Bush's response to the Los Angeles riots after the Rodney King verdict; Dallas *Morning News,* May 5, 1992

On Business

"GM has more talent, more money, more research capability, and more manufacturing facilities than any other car maker. Logically it should be first and best in building the finest cars in the world. It is not. GM has failed to tap the full potential of its resources, especially its people. This must be changed."
—*Fortune*, February 15, 1988

"Even in a bad year, the who's who of corporate America grants themselves enormous bonuses. It is obscene to have the gap between the factory floor and the corner office that we have."
—*The New York Times*, March 20, 1992

"Let me put it in military terms. If you go to war, you feed the troops before you feed the officers. Officers plan. Troops fight. If George Washington had been out buying new uniforms and gold braids, it would have been pretty hard to have motivated the troops. If we couldn't do anything for the guys who did the work, then we couldn't do anything for the guys who ran the place."
—Dallas *Morning News*, December 9, 1986

On Crime

"I make no distinction between the MBA white-collar criminal and the kid who is a high school

dropout who robs a 7-Eleven store, in terms of basic character. I mean the same basic character defect is in both people. The difference is of the highly polished package with your MBA."
—*Barron's,* February 23, 1987

On Drugs
"Simply declare civil war and the drug dealer is the enemy. There ain't no bail. You go straight to POW camp."
—*Fortune,* November 20, 1984

On the Economy
"It's outrageous that our elected officials say the fundamentals of the economy are sound; none of the fundamentals are sound. We have to ask, 'Whom are we hurting?' and recognize that we are leaving our children an unconscionable burden."
—*Newsweek,* November 2, 1987

"The only way to bulletproof our country is to design and make the best products in the world."
—*Fortune,* March 26, 1990

"We can't compete if our best and brightest young people are going to Wall Street to sell junk bonds. We can't compete if we don't have

strong leaders who will rebuild our companies
so they can make the finest products in the
world."
—*Fortune*, March 26, 1990

On Education

"You walk into an engineering school today and
you think you are in the Orient. Those aren't
Japanese-Americans in those classes—those are
Japanese, and they are flooding our schools.
We've got to change that; we've got to get
discipline and hard courses back for our
children."
—*Saturday Evening Post*, April 1983

"The public schools exist solely for the benefit of
the children. They do not exist for special
interests."
—Los Angeles *Times,* December 22, 1991

"Seventy-five percent of high school seniors
don't know who Whitman or Thoreau is.
Twenty-five percent of college seniors in Texas
can't name the country on Texas' southern
border. That's scary."
—*Texas Monthly*, December 1988

On the Federal Debt

"Have you ever heard the President talk about
the $4 trillion debt? I haven't. Have you ever

heard him come up with even a bad plan to work on it? I haven't. All you hear is Lawrence Welk music: wonnerful, wonnerful, wonnerful."
—Dallas *Morning News,* April 30, 1992; from a David Frost interview

"A pre-eminent economist whose name you would recognize immediately told me that there's at least $100 billion from people who get Medicare and Social Security who are so wealthy they don't need it."
—*Business Week,* April 27, 1992; quoted in the Dallas *Morning News,* April 30, 1992

On Foreign Policy
". . . the greatest thing that could happen to Israel in the Middle East is to have stability and peace. OK, my recommendation there is you put a world-class negotiating team over there, not flying back and forth. . . . Now you're looking for a cliff-climb here because the Middle East, by definition, is unstable."
—CNN Larry King interview; quoted in the Dallas *Morning News,* April 30, 1992

"If you don't like guys like [Panama General] Noriega, don't create them."
—*CBS Sunday Morning,* May 10, 1992

On Government

"The best kept secret in America: 1,200 private jets worth two billion [dollars] flying government officials around. See? These folks are our servants. They're flying around like royalty. What are they in such a hurry about? Why can't they fly and act like we do? OK, go to the airport, get in line, lose your luggage, eat a bad meal, have a taste of reality. Now, this is important."
—*60 Minutes,* March 29, 1992

"There are no sacred cows. You look at everything. If you don't think the unthinkable, then you really fail to look at opportunities."
—*Washington Post,* May 3, 1992

On Jobs

"When you try to create jobs in the public sector, you wind up adding to the tax burden, and this slows the economy."
—*Saturday Evening Post,* April 1983

"My concern is that a relatively small number of people in our country can develop the skills needed to create jobs. We have millions of people who are willing to work at a job, but a real shortage of people who know how to create jobs."
—*Barron's,* February 23, 1987

"If anybody will listen, I have said there is one priority that faces this country. That is to stop the decline in the job base. Because if we continue to lay off tens of thousands of people, we lose taxpayers and get welfare users. A welfare user gets more money from the government than a blue collar worker pays in taxes every month."
—*Newsweek*, April 27, 1992

On MIAs
"The President and the Vice President asked me to dig into this issue—go all the way to the bottom of it and figure out what the situation was—then come see them and give them my recommendation."
—Dallas *Morning News*, November 13, 1986

On Patriotism
"At some time in your life, you should give a year or two to your country. I wouldn't call it 'conscription.' I would call it 'service to country.' Every 18-year-old could work on jobs like conservation projects, hospital service or helping older people. It would have to have substance and be well organized."
—*Saturday Evening Post*, April 1983

"Well, we did recover Kuwait for the emir, but he ran like a rabbit when the war started. He

never touched it while it was dirty, and he would not come back into his own country until enlisted men from ordinary homes all over the United States cleaned up his palace and reinstalled his gold faucet fixtures. Now, let me say this. If I'm ever running the store and you see American enlisted men rebuilding a palace for an emir—you know, just have me shot and call it a mercy killing because, I mean, I've lost it. I've lost it. Seriously, seriously!"
—*60 Minutes*, March 29, 1992

"We're like the inheritors of great wealth in this country. We've forgotten all the sacrifices that the people who've gone before us made to give us this wonderful life that we have. We accept it, we take it for granted, we think it's our birthright. The facts are, it's precious, it's fragile, it can disappear on us in a moment. It's like quicksilver. If this is going to be a country that's owned by its people, then the owners have got to be active in the management of the country. It's that simple. The wimps are us."
—*Esquire*, June 1988

On Perot
"My family and friends get amused when they read that I'm severe because they think I have a great sense of humor and am rather informal."
—*Financial World*, August 8–21, 1984

"At this stage in my life, I do things for more than money."
—*Newsweek*, December 1, 1980

"I would rather try and fail than not try."
—*Time*, June 8, 1987

"But the most important thing my parents taught me is, do what's right and don't worry about what people think about it."
—*U.S. News & World Report*, June 20, 1988

"The people Norman Rockwell painted are my heroes."
—*Newsweek*, April 27, 1992

On the Presidency
"If and when I do this job, it will be because the American people come out of nowhere and put me in the job."
—*Newsweek*, April 27, 1992

"I didn't realize the system was this rotten. The thing that leaps out at you as a newcomer is that the process to select a President is totally irrelevant and disconnected from selecting a good person. It has everything to do with sound bites, whispers and innuendoes."
—*Newsweek*, April 27, 1992

"The one thing I know at this point, if I get stuck up there, I can't stay inside the [Washington, D.C.] Beltway. It's like living in a bubble. If you don't see, feel and taste the real America, you could be up there and not know there's a recession."
—*Newsweek*, April 27, 1992

"If they [the voters] like a President who shreds, runs, ducks and hides and tries to blame minor officials, they don't want me because I will take responsibility for my actions."
—Dallas *Morning News*, April 30, 1992; from a David Frost interview

"It's time to take out the trash and clean out the barn."
—*Newsweek*, March 30, 1992

On the Rodney King Case

"When I saw that tape the thing that just leaped at me, number one, was the shock that a group of men would do that. The second, I couldn't believe that the other guys didn't stop it. See, typically, in a situation like this, one person loses it, but then the others go in and pull him off, and that didn't happen. So the sad thing is—the tragic thing is that it could happen, then I—to me, we've got to get to the bottom of how trained people could all

participate in that. What forces caused them to be that way. Then you look at the end result, the verdict, which I can't understand the verdict. Now you have the problem."
—*Meet the Press*, May 3, 1992

On the Savings and Loan Crisis
"There was a lot of crooked stuff, and I'd put a lot of these guys in jail."
—Dallas *Morning News,* November 18, 1988

On Taxes
"Bad highways and bridges are a drain on our economy, and it is vital that they are rebuilt. The gasoline tax is an indirect form of a toll road. The road user pays through this tax. I don't have a better idea for raising the money needed for this vital work, so until one comes along, I'll have to go along with it. There's not enough money in general revenue to pay for the rebuilding."
—*Saturday Evening Post,* April 1983

"If we have to raise taxes, OK. Everyone is going to have to take his or her share of the hit. It's better to recover from a drinking habit before you lose your liver."
—*Newsweek,* November 2, 1987

CHAPTER 5

PEROT'S VISION OF AMERICA

"I ignore any kidding about my love of country. My interest in this country is deep, complex, and very well thought out. Simply put, we just can't take from our country, we must also give. It is easy to criticize the dirty river. It's a challenge to clean it up."—Ross Perot
Saturday Evening Post; April 1983

Opposite: Perot has a deep love for America and is convinced he has the vision to lead the nation effectively.

Can Ross Perot succeed in his quixotic adventure? In the past he's taken on Iranian bullies, General Motors bureaucrats, and some of Texas's most powerful people: high school football coaches. His current quest, however, dwarfs all his previous exploits.

If Perot succeeds, he will be the first President ever elected without the aid of an existing political party. If he runs the tough, honest campaign he has promised, he could gain the gratitude of millions of voters even if he fails. If he doesn't live up to the high standards he has promised—in other words, if he runs a conventional campaign full of empty promises, mudslinging, and media stunts—he will lose, and lose in a way that will tarnish his reputation and cost him the good will of the American people. Clearly, Ross Perot has put much more than his money on the line in this race.

Perot has said he loves challenges. He's happiest, he has said, when the critics are counting him out. It's good that he loves a challenge, because history shows that Perot faces an arduous uphill climb. Although the two

---

Chris Tucker is a columnist and editor for D
Magazine *and a long-time Perot-watcher. Tucker interviewed Ross Perot in mid-April and again in early May of 1992. This chapter is based on those interviews as well as Tucker's own observations of Perot.*

Grass-roots activism characterizes Perot's presidential campaign, as volunteers respond to his plain talk.

major political parties are weaker today than at any time in U.S. history, the very nature of American politics still favors the two-party system.

In the past, the two major parties have responded to challenges from independents by reaching out and co-opting the issues that concerned the voters. In 1968, George Wallace argued that "there was not a dime's worth of difference" between the Republicans and the Democrats. He charged that both parties had abandoned the white middle class and demanded that campus demonstrators and urban "Black Power" militants be curbed.

Perot met George Bush at a May 1990 Patrick Henry
Foundation function held in Perot's honor.

Wallace got about 10 percent of the vote,
the largest total in 44 years for a third-party
candidate. He would have taken more had not
the Republican party adopted much of
Wallace's rhetoric in building Richard Nixon's
"law and order" platform. If Ross Perot
continues to show well in the polls, look for
George Bush and Bill Clinton to sound more
and more like clones of him.

There is also the problem of the fickle
public. Polls around the country show Perot
grabbing anywhere from 20 to 33 percent of the
vote. But Perot underwent three months of
saturation coverage from the media before he

even declared for President—the most attention
ever paid to an undeclared candidate and more,
no doubt, than many senators and congressmen
have enjoyed during long careers in
Washington. Inevitably, this has raised hopes
sky-high among Perot supporters and increased
expectations among the millions of American
voters who are eager to learn more about Perot's
ideas for solving the nation's problems.

The danger exists for Perot that people could
come to expect too much of him, and then
judge him harshly when he falls short. In
Dallas, a joke has been circulating for weeks:
Seems that Ross Perot got up and went out for
his morning walk; everything was fine until he
got hit by a boat. If people come to believe that
Perot can walk on water before he even spells
out his platform, a small gaffe or misstatement
could do him great damage.

But Perot, as he has shown throughout his
life, is anything but a helpless pawn. Any
challenger who goes into battle without the
weapons of the Democratic or Republican party
arsenals must bring firepower of his own, and
Perot has powerful weapons at his disposal.
They include many that are already obvious,
and many more that will emerge as the
campaign gathers steam. Under the media
microscope, Perot will be shown to have his
share of warts and flaws. Taken together,
however, Perot's ideas, deeds, and qualities yield
a vision of America that may inspire millions.

Much of Perot's vision is rooted in small town America and in the lessons he learned during his boyhood.

Confidence. Perot, as a Dallas newspaper columnist once put it, long ago banished the word "can't" from his vocabulary. He's typically American in that he favors blunt, concise action plans over elaborately footnoted theories. "You can always find ten ways to prove something can't be done," Perot said. "The trick is finding one way it can be done." Perot's unshakable belief in himself can shade over into arrogance, but it's an arrogance people understand, based on solid accomplishments.

Wealth and Independence. In American politics, a vast fortune is a double-edged sword. Some rich candidates have been tagged as elitist dandies who were out of touch with the masses. But great wealth is not an automatic curse to a politician: The Kennedys, despite their wealth, became populist spokesmen for the little guy, and several Rockefellers have been elected to office. Much depends on whether the wealth was inherited or earned. Perot's story—small town boy gets big idea, makes billions—is close to the Horatio Alger stuff of American legend. The average Joe can respect a man who worked his way up, even if it's way up to the stratosphere. Besides, Perot lives about as unostentatiously as a billionaire can, shopping at discount stores and driving a late model station wagon. He can deflect criticism of his wealth by repeating his belief that any higher taxes should start with those in his income bracket. He also believes that the very rich should not receive Medicare or Social Security benefits.

"There are a lot of us that have been very fortunate in this country," Perot stated. "We can pay for it, and we don't need federal money to do it."

Most important, Perot's fortune grants him independence from pressure groups and frees him from what politicians say is the bane of their existence: fund-raising. Perot needs no contributors to pay his way. At a time when voters are fed up with special interests who lobby their way to power, Perot can write his own check and call his own tune. He won't even accept federal matching funds. That financial independence should serve him well with voters.

Strength and Toughness. It has been noted for decades that voters reject candidates whom

American voters are searching for answers and plain truth; Perot is prepared to provide them with both.

they consider "soft" on national defense issues. Even with the Soviet Union's collapse, Americans are likely to continue insisting that the President be ready to flex America's military muscle when the cause is just.

While Perot is no reckless saber rattler, he is certainly nobody's idea of a pacifist. Although he opposed the Persian Gulf War on the grounds that no real American interest was at stake, opponents will have a hard time painting him as antimilitary. He served four years in the peacetime Navy. Beyond that, he has amassed more "foreign policy" experience, or its rough equivalent, than many who have sought the presidency.

Perot first gained widespread public attention with his Christmas 1969 mission to North Vietnam, trying to deliver supplies and mail to American POWs. The image that stuck was of a private businessman spending his own money to help those who had sacrificed for America. And over the years, Perot has spent millions of his own dollars searching for American soldiers he believes are still being held in Vietnam. The most famous episode in Perot's foreign-policy dossier is the 1979 Iran rescue mission of two EDS employees. Critics scolded Perot for raising a "private army" and meddling in another country's affairs, but the Iran mission impressed the majority of Americans as the bold, magnanimous act of a leader. Legal niceties aside, the average voter will have little trouble answering this question: "If I am stuck in a foreign prison in the middle of a revolution, what should my boss do?"

The Courage To Tell the Hard Truth. If he stays true to his word, Perot is going to run the straight-talking, no-nonsense campaign that so many voters say they want—the type of campaign Paul Tsongas went broke trying to do. Perot won't go broke. But do voters really want the blunt truth, even if it means sacrifice in the form of spending cuts or higher taxes?

The question, in political terms, is: Who is to blame for the $400 billion deficit and the $4 trillion national debt? Perot has sent mixed signals on this score. Part of the time he takes

As Perot's campaign has developed, he has drawn more
enthusiastic crowds. Whether by motorcade . . .

the easy way out—blaming everything on the
greedy hogs at the Capitol Hill trough and
talking as if the rest of us are just innocent
bystanders. At other times, however, Perot has
come close to doing something few politicians
have the courage to do: telling voters that the
party's over and that it's time to pay the check.
The hard truth, Perot knows, is that the people
created the divided, gridlocked government we
now curse. The people also helped inflate the
budget deficit by demanding that Washington
fund innumerable pork-barrel projects.

Perot also insists on more personal
responsibility concerning education. Our

. . . or via press-the-flesh encounters, Perot is making a
startling impact on voters.

schools, he said, will not be improved merely by
restructuring the bureaucracy or raising
teachers' salaries.

"The greatest legacy we could leave our kids
is the best educational system in the world,"
Perot stated. "But if parents don't go to PTA
meetings, don't know who's on the school
board, nothing will happen. And if you don't
study with that little character when he gets
home, no amount of money is going to help."

Much the same conviction lies behind
Perot's opinions on abortion, one of the most
controversial topics a politician can tackle. He
supports a woman's right to choose abortion,

The boxes seen here contain signed petitions intended to get Perot's name on the presidential ballot in Texas.

but adds, "it's more complicated than just saying it's all the woman's right. We're not rabbits, we're thinking human beings. We don't have to create a life we don't want. If people don't want to hear that from me, they don't want me in Washington."

Perot said he will continue telling people to "look in the mirror" to see who's responsible for our problems and who can solve them. "We're the owners of this country, and we've got to start acting like it," he said. What if people don't want to hear that kind of talk? "I don't care. It's something I believe." For Perot, ownership implies responsibility, and Perot has

The words may be uncompromising, but voters sense an honesty that makes Perot's messages palatable.

the courage to keep holding up that mirror to reflect that responsibility.

"Tough Love" for America. The thorniest dilemma for politicians is this: How to get voters to face real problems without making them feel guilty and, ultimately, resentful of the messenger? Perot's words and deeds over the years have put him in a position to tell those hard truths without alienating the electorate.

People will listen to criticism and calls for sacrifice from politicians, but the alarm must be sounded by a leader whose love of country cannot be questioned. Voters may not know

Perot meets admirers in Austin, Texas, in May of 1992.
He feels a deep kinship with ordinary Americans.

where Perot stands on strip mining or aid to
Ecuador, but they do know that his patriotic
credentials cannot be questioned. In the trench
warfare of the campaign, Perot will be
vulnerable to attack on a number of fronts, but
the Republican party will not be able to
question his patriotism as they did with
Democratic presidential candidate Michael
Dukakis in 1988.

Perot's love of country is clearly an
uncalculated, genuine thing. For years he has
delighted in showing visitors his Dallas office,
which is a veritable shrine to traditional

At that Austin appearance, Perot hammered home his message about the people's ability to effect change.

American virtues and values. He's proud to own the famed "Spirit of '76" painting, along with some Frederic Remington bronzes and several originals by Norman Rockwell, Perot's favorite painter. Perot said he bought the paintings because they illustrate central truths about his country and his own life.

One of the Rockwells, "Homecoming Marine," depicts a young Marine who has returned to the auto shop where he worked

Eligible voters sign ballot petitions at a May 1992 Perot drive in Santa Barbara, California.

before the war. Older men listen, beaming with pride, as he tells his war stories. For Perot, the painting represents the American spirit at its best.

"It's ordinary people doing extraordinary things," he said.

Perot believes in the nobler aspect of everyday Americans. His message has not been lost on voters.

"A few weeks or months ago, that boy was fighting for his country and his buddies. Now he's back, and in a few days he'll be fixing flats again. That's what Americans do, and that's what makes our country great. [French political scientist] de Tocqueville said that America is great because her people are good, and if our people ever cease to be good, America will cease to be great."

Another Rockwell painting, "Breaking Home Ties," has a more personal meaning for Perot. The painting shows a father waiting with his son for the train that will take the boy off to college. "That's the story of my life in that

Perot's critics insist that his ideas are unworkable because of their inherent simplicity. Perot begs to differ.

painting," Perot said. "My father was a very smart man, but he was forced to drop out of school at 14 because he had to work."

Perot's parents were determined that he and his sister go to college and made their dream come true. Perot is not given to introspection, but it's not hard to see that his parents' sacrifice helped form his personal philosophy.

Perot fears that the discipline and work ethic that drove his parents has declined in importance today. "Our parents worked and sacrificed so that we could have better lives," he said. To Perot, the deficit is the most potent symbol of our lost direction: "We've spent our children's money," he said, and fell into uncommon silence.

Perot's supporters are unmoved by anti-Perot sentiment. This rally featured a balloon saying "So Long, Bush."

Until Election Day, critics will complain that Ross Perot's vision of America is overly simple, antiquated, and out of touch with the reality of our sprawling, troubled urban centers. In some ways, the critics are right. No politician has the magic bullet for every problem. If the standard

Commitment. Dedication. Hard work. Ross Perot says
he's ready.

is perfection, then the New Deal, the Great
Society, and the New World Order all fall short.

Perot's vision is undeniably simple. But does
simple mean wrong? At the heart of it, Perot
believes that, despite the government's
labyrinthine complexity and the problems that
have baffled so many experts, the nation still
belongs to the people if they are willing to do
the hard work of democracy.

"I can't do it all," he said. "No one person
can do it all. What I'm saying is that if people
will not just vote and go home . . . but get in the
ring and stay in the ring after November, we
can fix these problems."

That may be what people sense in Ross
Perot's campaign: a fighting chance to make it
work—if people get involved and stay involved.